200 Italian f[avourites]

Kerrie

hamlyn | all colour cookbook
200 Italian favourites

Marina Filippelli

An Hachette UK Company
www.hachette.co.uk

First published in Great Britain in 2009 by Hamlyn,
a division of Octopus Publishing Group Ltd
2–4 Heron Quays, London E14 4JP
www.octopusbooks.co.uk

Copyright © Octopus Publishing Group Ltd 2009

Some of the recipes in this book have previously appeared in other books published by Hamlyn.

All rights reserved. No part of this work may be reproduced or utilized in any form or by any means, electronic or mechanical, including photocopying, recording or by any information storage and retrieval system, without the prior written permission of the publisher.

ISBN: 978-0-600-61936-9

A CIP catalogue record for this book is available from the British Library

Printed and bound in China

1 2 3 4 5 6 7 8 9 10

Both metric and imperial measurements have been given in all recipes. Use one set of measurements only, and not a mixture of both.

Standard level spoon measurements are used in all recipes.
1 tablespoon = one 15 ml spoon
1 teaspoon = one 5 ml spoon

Ovens should be preheated to the specified temperature – if using a fan-assisted oven, follow the manufacturer's instructions for adjusting the time and the temperature.

Fresh herbs should be used unless otherwise stated.

Medium eggs should be used unless otherwise stated.

The Department of Health advises that eggs should not be consumed raw. This book contains some dishes made with raw or lightly cooked eggs. It is prudent for vulnerable people such as pregnant and nursing mothers, invalids, the elderly, babies and young children to avoid uncooked or lightly cooked dishes made with eggs. Once prepared, these dishes should be kept refrigerated and used promptly.

This book includes dishes made with nuts and nut derivatives. It is advisable for those with known allergic reactions to nuts and nut derivatives and those who may be potentially vulnerable to these allergies, such as pregnant and nursing mothers, invalids, the elderly, babies and children, to avoid dishes made with nuts and nut oils. It is also prudent to check the labels of pre-prepared ingredients for the possible inclusion of nut derivatives.

contents

introduction	6
antipasti & salads	16
pasta & pizza	52
soups, rice & polenta	90
fish & seafood	126
meat & poultry	150
vegetables & legumes	178
desserts	202
index	236
acknowledgements	240

introduction

introduction

Italian food is now so popular that classics such as lasagne or tiramisu have become household favourites in all corners of the world. Fuss-free homely food, fresh ingredients and simple techniques all make for a cuisine that has instant appeal to the modern cook. Anybody can cook Italian, and whether you are throwing together a quick pasta dish or letting a stew slowly simmer on the hob, the beauty of Italian cooking is that most dishes don't demand a lot of preparation time. For this reason, having a good repertoire of dishes to hand can be a lifesaver for busy weekday family meals and for entertaining alike.

eating the Italian way

Italians love their food so much that the dining table is the hub of the family. Breakfast generally consists of a cappuccino or espresso with biscuits or a *brioche*, which in Italy is more like a croissant. Lunch and dinner are not dissimilar in their structure. Traditionally, they are split into four courses: *antipasto*, *primo piatto*, *secondo piatto* and the *dolce*. The *antipasto* (starter) can be either one dish or a combination of several small dishes, served tapas-style and referred to in the plural as *antipasti*. Then comes the *primo piatto* (first course), which may be pasta, soup, risotto or polenta, depending on personal and regional preferences. The *secondo piatto* (second course) is a meat or fish dish

accompanied by vegetables or salad. Finally comes the *dolce* (dessert), which is hardly ever skipped but often only consists of a simple fruit salad or a bowl of fruit taken to the table for everyone to tuck into. Bread and wine are a constant at the Italian table and most people complete their meal with a shot of espresso.

Nowadays, not all Italian meals consist of so many courses. Frequently, just a pasta and a meat dish are served, followed by a fruit, or a bowl of pasta, then a vegetable side dish. A heavy lunch could be followed by just a wholesome soup, such as minestrone, for dinner. Whatever the meal, however, it is unlikely that an Italian will ever leave the table having eaten only a huge bowl of pasta or a large steak – that just wouldn't constitute a properly balanced meal and they have too healthy a relationship with food for that.

regional favourites

Italians often argue that there is no such thing as Italian food but rather lots of regional culinary traditions. Fresh pasta, for instance, is a northern dish and is hardly ever eaten in southern Italy. In the south, cooks exclusively use olive oil, while in the first half of the 20th century butter was the cooking medium of choice in the north. The divisions used to be distinct: pizza, tomatoes, mozzarella cheese and chilli belonged to the south, while risotto, cream and black pepper were essentially northern. Today, the borders are blurred and favourite regional ingredients and dishes have become popular throughout the country and beyond. The recipes in this book represent family favourites from all over the country. Most are traditional, while some are inspired by contemporary flavour combinations.

the Italian larder

The Italian cook depends on a well-stocked larder. Most of these ingredients are available in supermarkets, with only the more unusual ones requiring a trip to an Italian deli.

anchovies

Most commonly used in southern cooking, anchovies can be bought fresh or preserved in salt or oil. Salted anchovies taste fresher than those preserved in oil, but will need thorough rinsing to remove the salt. The flavour and saltiness of preserved anchovies can be mellowed by soaking them in milk. The recipes here use the preserved fish.

capers

These small flower buds are preserved in salt or brine. Rinse thoroughly in cold water to remove the saltiness or sharpness from the vinegar before using. Small capers are generally more flavoursome than larger buds.

cheeses

Mozzarella This can be made from cows' milk or water buffaloes' milk (*mozzarella di bufala*). Cows' milk mozzarella is more than adequate to use in cooking when it is going to be melted, but if you are planning to eat your mozzarella fresh, for instance in a tomato and mozzarella salad, it is worth splashing out on buffalo mozzarella, which tastes creamier. Only buy mozzarella kept in water.

Parmesan *Parmigiano Reggiano* is a cows' milk cheese made in the Emilia-Romagna region of northern Italy. It is used extensively, grated on to pasta, stirred into risottos or shaved on to salads. It is also delicious broken into small pieces and eaten as a nibble with a glass of red wine. *Grana Padano* is similar to Parmesan and makes a more economical choice for use in cooking.

Pecorino This sheep's milk cheese is made in central and southern Italy. There are different varieties, which can be aged until they are ready for the table or matured further until dry and crumbly, to be used grated in cooking.

Ricotta This is a naturally low-fat soft cheese made from the whey left over from cheese making. The whey is reheated, then strained into baskets to drain, hence the name *ricotta*, which literally means 'recooked'. The most commonly found ricotta outside Italy is made from cows' milk and it is the one recommended for the recipes in this book.

Fontina This is a mild cheese from Piedmont, which melts evenly and smoothly, making it perfect for cooking. You can find it in good supermarkets and delis.

Gorgonzola and dolcelatte Both these blue cheeses are often used in pasta sauces. Gorgonzola is the strongest, comparable to Stilton or Roquefort. Dolcelatte is much creamier, with a milder, more delicate flavour.
Mascarpone A full-fat, very thick cream cheese with a rich, smooth texture and mild flavour, which is famously used in the classic dessert, tiramisu.

hams

Prosciutto is the generic Italian word for ham. *Prosciutto crudo* (literally meaning 'raw ham') is the most commonly known Italian ham, of which the most famous variety is *Prosciutto di Parma* (Parma ham). It is a raw ham cured in salt, then hung to dry and age. What makes Parma ham so special is that it is made with the hind legs of pigs fed on the whey left over from producing Parmesan cheese, making it sweeter than other *prosciutti crudi*. *Prosciutto cotto* is cooked ham. Speck, a smoke-cured ham from the northern borders of Italy, is also used in some of the recipes. It has a robust, smoky flavour and can be found in most delis and supermarkets. Black Forest ham can be used as an alternative.

olive oil

There are different grades of olive oil. Extra virgin olive oil is made from the first cold pressing of olives and its rich flavour can vary from peppery to nutty or grassy. For best results, it is essential to use extra virgin in recipes where the oil is not cooked or where it features as one of the main ingredients.

Regular, commercially produced and less expensive olive oil can be used in recipes where the oil is used for frying or sautéing vegetables at the beginning of cooking.

pasta

Pasta is eaten throughout Italy, with different regions favouring different shapes and sauces. It can be made with or without egg, using durum wheat and/or soft wheat flour and eaten fresh or dried. Italians have strong opinions regarding which pasta to use with which sauce, and there are many exceptions to the general rule. Your best guide to making the appropriate choice is tradition, so go with what recipes suggest and what you see being used in restaurants in Italy. Buy the best you can afford and choose authentic Italian brands.

People often hold the misconception that fresh pasta is superior or somehow more sophisticated than dried pasta. This couldn't be further from the truth. Fresh pasta is reserved for specific shapes and sauces and is most frequently eaten in central and northern Italy. In certain regions of southern Italy, such as the island of Sicily, people who eat pasta every day might never even have tasted it fresh!

polenta

This coarsely ground corn flour is cooked in water to the consistency of mashed potatoes and served with meat or squid in a sauce. Once cold, soft polenta sets into a rigid block that can be topped with other ingredients and grilled. It takes about 40 minutes to cook polenta, but you can get very good results with the instant polenta most Italians use in everyday cooking. It takes just five minutes to cook instant polenta, and therefore is the favoured variety for the recipes in this book.

pulses

Borlotti beans, cannellini beans, chickpeas and lentils are very popular in Italian soups, stews and salads. Beans and chickpeas are eaten fresh when in season, but when cooking them from dry, they will need soaking overnight in cold water. Canned pulses, rinsed, can be used if time is short. You will need twice the quantity of canned beans to dried, so if a recipe calls for 100 g (3½ oz) dried borlotti beans, for example, use 200 g (7 oz) rinsed canned borlotti beans. Italians often save time by cooking with canned beans and as a result their brands are generally of an outstanding quality, so are well worth searching out.

risotto rice

This is now readily available in supermarkets and delis, so there is no need to attempt making risotto with any other rice. Avoid generically labelled risotto rice and opt instead for one of three specific varieties grown in the Po Valley: arborio, carnaroli and vialone nano. Stirring risotto as it cooks helps the grains release their starch and it is this stirring that makes the final result so creamy.

tomatoes

There is an abundance of tomatoes of every different kind available in Italy in summer, from juicy plum tomatoes to sweet cherry tomatoes and green salad tomatoes. Each variety has its own use, and San Marzano plum tomatoes are prized for making sauces. These are the tomatoes most commonly used peeled in cans, chopped or whole. Good-quality canned tomatoes should not be frowned upon and Italians happily use them in winter to make their sauces. In fact, you are better off using canned tomatoes than unripened acidic greenhouse tomatoes any day! Passata is smooth, raw puréed tomatoes sold bottled or in cartons to use in cooking.

mushrooms

The most widely available wild mushrooms in Italy are porcini, chanterelles and girolles. During their short season in late summer and autumn, they are eaten raw in salads, pan-fried with garlic and stirred into pasta, eaten on *bruschette* or polenta, used in risottos or served with sliced steak. Any other time of the year, Italians rely on dried mushrooms that need soaking in hot water before cooking. Of these, porcini are the most popular, stirred into stews, soups and risottos, and delicious pan-fried with the most mundane field mushrooms. Make sure you use the soaking water from mushrooms, as it is packed with flavour.

vinegar

Red wine vinegar is the most commonly used vinegar for both dressing salads and cooking. Balsamic vinegar, made in Modena, is also popular but it is only really worth buying good-quality aged balsamic that should be rich, sweet and syrupy. The real thing can be very pricey, but a little goes a long way with balsamic vinegar and just a few drops are enough to enliven a salad, sauce or even a bowl of fresh strawberries.

recommended equipment

All the recipes in this book are technically quite straightforward, so don't call for very specialized equipment. A well-stocked kitchen with chopping boards, sharp knives and a range of different sized pans and baking tins is all you'll need, while the list below suggests a few useful extras.

large saucepan

You cannot cook pasta properly in a small saucepan. You will need a pan large enough so that the pasta has plenty of space to move around in the boiling water while cooking, to avoid it sticking to the base of the pan.

colander
Once your pasta has been cooked until tender but still firm to the bite, or *al dente*, you need to drain it very quickly. For this purpose, a large colander that you can sit in your sink is much more efficient than a sieve.

tongs
These useful utensils make it easy to serve long pasta such as spaghetti or linguine or to toss it into a sauce. They are also great for turning over meats or vegetables when frying or griddling.

nonstick frying pan
This is not strictly essential but can be extremely helpful when trying to cut down on the quantity of oil or butter used in cooking. The best frying pans have a heavy base and a solid, ovenproof handle.

ridged griddle pan
Griddling is a great way of cooking steaks, chops, chicken breasts, chunky fish steaks and vegetables without the need for oil. The pan needs to be heated until smoking hot to sear the ingredients quickly and achieve the desired charred flavour and griddle marks.

mouli or ricer
One or other of these items is essential for achieving the light, fluffy, lump-free mash needed for gnocchi. Even if you don't make gnocchi very often, these cheap tools can be used for any recipe where ingredients need to be mashed.

techniques
Most of the techniques used are explained clearly in the relevant recipes in the book. However, to avoid unnecessary repetition in the many recipes for shellfish and seafood, here are some basic instructions on how to prepare them for cooking:

cleaning mussels
Scrub mussels under cold running water. Pull away the 'beards' and discard any open shells that are broken or any that remain open when tapped. Soak in plenty of cold water for 30 minutes, then drain and rinse again in cold running water. Put in a bowl, cover with a wet tea towel and keep refrigerated until needed.

cleaning clams
Wash the clams under cold running water, discarding any that are broken or that remain open when tapped. Soak in plenty of cold water for 30 minutes, then drain and rinse them again in cold running water. Place in a bowl, cover with a wet tea towel and keep refrigerated until needed.

cleaning squid
Wash the squid under cold running water. Pull the tentacles away from the body. The squid's entrails will come out easily. Remove the clear piece of cartilage inside the body cavity and discard. Wash the body thoroughly, pulling away the pinkish membrane. Cut between the tentacles and head, discarding the head and entrails. Most fishmongers will be happy to take care of this messy job for you.

basic pizza dough

Makes **4**
Preparation time **15 minutes**, plus rising

7 g (¼ oz) **fresh yeast** or 1 teaspoon **fast-action dried yeast**
pinch of **caster sugar**
500 g (1 lb) **plain flour**, plus extra for dusting
350 ml (12 fl oz) **lukewarm water**
1½ teaspoons **salt**

Dissolve the yeast in a bowl with the sugar, 2 tablespoons of the flour and 50 ml (2 fl oz) of the measurement water. Leave to stand for 5 minutes until the mixture starts to form bubbles, then add the remaining water. Add the salt and half the remaining flour and stir with one hand until you have a paste-like mixture. Gradually add all the remaining flour, working the mixture until you have a moist dough.

Shape the dough into a ball, cover with a moist cloth and leave to rest in a warm place for 5 minutes.

Lightly dust a work surface with flour and knead the dough for 10 minutes until smooth and elastic. Shape into 4 equal-sized balls and place, spaced apart, on a lightly oiled tray. Cover with a moist cloth and leave to rise in a warm place for 1 hour. Use according to the particular recipe.

antipasti & salads

fried vegetables in batter

Serves **6**
Preparation time **15 minutes**
Cooking time **15 minutes**

100 g (3½ oz) **cauliflower**
100 g (3½ oz) **broccoli**
1 **red pepper**
1 **courgette**
1 **onion**
75 g (3 oz) **plain flour**, for dusting
sunflower oil, for deep-frying
6 **flat leaf parsley sprigs**
salt and **pepper**

Batter
2 **eggs**, lightly beaten
1 tablespoon **olive oil**
300 ml (½ pint) **chilled lager**
pinch of **salt**
225 g (7½ oz) **plain flour**, sifted

Combine all the ingredients for the batter in a large bowl, mixing well but not worrying about any lumps that may have formed. Cover and chill while you prepare the vegetables.

Cut the cauliflower and broccoli into small florets. Core and deseed the pepper, then cut it lengthways into 8 strips. Slice the courgette into 1 cm (½ inch) rounds and cut the onion into 8 wedges. Tip the flour into a bowl and season with salt and pepper, then toss in the prepared vegetables.

Heat enough oil for deep-frying in a deep saucepan to 180–190°C (350–375°F), or until a cube of bread browns in 30 seconds. Take 5 or 6 vegetable pieces from the flour, shake off any excess, then plunge into the batter. Lift out, letting the batter drip off slightly, then carefully plunge into the hot oil. Cook for about 3 minutes until golden. Remove with a slotted spoon and drain on kitchen paper. Once all the vegetables are cooked, lightly dust the parsley sprigs with flour, dip in the batter and cook for 1–2 minutes, or until just golden.

Season the vegetables and parsley with salt and serve immediately.

For basil & lemon batter, make the batter as above, but add the grated rind of 1 lemon and 3 tablespoons chopped basil. Cover and leave to infuse in the refrigerator for at least 30 minutes before using as above. The parsley sprigs can be replaced with 8 drained anchovy fillets in olive oil.

porcini bruschetta with truffle oil

Serves **4**
Preparation time **10 minutes**
Cooking time **5 minutes**

4 thick slices of **country bread**
2 **garlic cloves**, bruised
extra virgin olive oil, for drizzling
2 tablespoons chopped **flat leaf parsley**, plus extra to garnish
4 small **fresh porcini (ceps)**
lemon juice, for drizzling
truffle oil, for drizzling
salt and **pepper**

Toast the bread slices on both sides under a preheated medium grill or in a preheated ridged griddle pan or over a barbecue. Rub 1 side of each toasted slice with the bruised garlic, then drizzle with the oil and sprinkle with the parsley.

Pick over the porcini and brush off any grit. Remove the stalks and thinly slice. Slice the caps as thinly as possible.

Cut the toasted slices in half. Scatter over the sliced porcini stalks, drizzle with a little lemon juice and season with salt and pepper. Cover with the sliced porcini caps. Drizzle with more lemon juice and a little truffle oil, season again with pepper and garnish with a little chopped parsley. Serve immediately.

For Parmesan, porcini & radicchio bruschetta, prepare the bruschetta as above, omitting the parsley and lemon and dividing a handful of shredded radicchio leaves between each bread slice before adding the mushrooms. Top each bruschetta with a couple of Parmesan shavings, season with salt and pepper and drizzle with extra virgin olive oil instead of the truffle oil.

rocket & garlic crumbed mussels

Serves **4**
Preparation time **15 minutes**
Cooking time **10 minutes**

25 g (1 oz) **wild rocket leaves**
1 **garlic clove**
50 g (2 oz) **fresh white breadcrumbs**
4 tablespoons **extra virgin olive oil**
1 kg (2 lb) **mussels**, cleaned (see page 14)
salt and **pepper**
lemon wedges, to serve

Process the rocket and garlic in a food processor until roughly chopped. Add the breadcrumbs and pulse until combined, then stir in the oil. Season with salt and pepper. Cover and chill until needed.

Put the mussels in a large saucepan with a tight-fitting lid and add water to a depth of 2.5 cm (1 inch). Cover and bring to the boil over a high heat. Cook the mussels, shaking the pan frequently, for 2–3 minutes, or until the shells have opened. Drain, discarding any that remain closed. Pull away and discard the empty shell halves, reserving only the halves with the mussels attached.

Place the mussels, flesh-side up, on a baking sheet. Divide the breadcrumb topping between the mussels and cook on the top shelf of a preheated high grill for 1–2 minutes until the breadcrumbs are golden. Serve immediately with lemon wedges on the side.

For tomato & parsley crumbed scallops, make the breadcrumb mixture as above, but replace the rocket with 20 g (¾ oz) flat leaf parsley and 4 drained sun-dried tomatoes in oil. Instead of the mussels, use 12 opened scallops. Loosen the scallops from their base shell by cutting through the muscle that attaches them to the shell with a small, sharp knife. Divide the breadcrumb topping between the scallops and cook under the grill as above, but increase the cooking time to 2–3 minutes.

broad bean bruschetta

Serves **4**
Preparation time **15 minutes**
Cooking time **3 minutes**

5 tablespoons **extra virgin olive oil**, plus extra for drizzling
2 **garlic cloves**, 1 crushed and 1 left whole
pinch of **crushed dried chillies**
handful of **mint leaves**
250 g (8 oz) shelled **broad beans**, thawed if frozen, skins removed
40 g (1½ oz) **Pecorino cheese**, grated
1 small **ciabatta loaf**, cut into 8 thin slices
salt and **pepper**
Parmesan cheese shavings, to serve

Combine the oil, crushed garlic, crushed chillies and mint in a bowl and leave to infuse for 10 minutes.

Meanwhile, lightly crush the broad beans in a separate bowl with a fork. Season with salt and pepper, then toss into the oil mixture with the Pecorino. Toast the bread slices on both sides under a preheated medium grill or in a preheated ridged griddle pan or over a barbecue.

Rub the toasted slices with the remaining garlic. Top with the broad bean mixture and drizzle over a little oil. Scatter with Parmesan shavings and serve immediately.

For Parmesan & cannellini bean bruschetta, combine 2 crushed garlic cloves, 1 teaspoon chopped rosemary and 4 tablespoons extra virgin olive oil in a bowl and leave to infuse for 10 minutes. Drain a 400 g (13 oz) can cannellini beans, rinse, then drain again. Lightly crush with a fork and stir into the oil mixture with 2 tablespoons freshly grated Parmesan cheese, salt to taste and a large pinch of crushed dried chillies. Serve on toasted bread slices, as above, drizzled with a little extra oil and scattered with Parmesan shavings.

carpaccio of fresh tuna

Serves **4**
Preparation time **10 minutes**, plus freezing

250 g (8 oz) piece of **tuna loin**
juice of 3 **lemons**
150 ml (¼ pint) **extra virgin olive oil**
1 **garlic clove**, finely chopped
1 tablespoon **salted capers**, rinsed
125 g (4 oz) **wild rocket leaves**
salt and **pepper**
Parmesan cheese shavings, to serve

Trim the tuna of any membrane or gristle. Wrap tightly in clingfilm and put in the freezer for about 1 hour until just frozen but not rock solid.

Meanwhile, whisk together the lemon juice, oil, garlic and capers in a bowl. Add salt and pepper to taste and whisk until emulsified.

Unwrap the tuna and thinly slice with a sharp, thin-bladed knife. Arrange the slices on 4 large serving plates. Spoon the dressing over the tuna. Top with a tangle of rocket leaves and scatter with Parmesan shavings.

For fresh swordfish carpaccio, replace the tuna with 250 g (8 oz) piece of swordfish. Freeze, thinly slice and arrange on plates as above. Whisk together the lemon juice, olive oil and garlic, also adding 2 tablespoons chopped flat leaf parsley, instead of the capers. Spoon over the plated fish and top with the rocket. Omit the Parmesan cheese.

balsamic figs with parma ham

Serves **4**
Preparation time **5 minutes**
Cooking time **4–5 minutes**

8 **ripe fresh figs**
2 tablespoons **balsamic vinegar**
extra virgin olive oil, for drizzling
12 slices of **Parma ham**
50 g (2 oz) **wild rocket leaves**
salt and **pepper**

Cut the figs in half and arrange, cut-side up, on a baking sheet. Brush with the vinegar and lightly drizzle with oil. Season with a little salt and a generous grinding of pepper.

Cook under a preheated high grill for 4–5 minutes until heated through and a little charred.

Arrange 3 slices of Parma ham on each serving plate. Top with the grilled figs and scatter with rocket leaves. Drizzle over a little more oil and serve while the figs are still warm.

For minted melon with Parma ham, put a sliced small, ripe melon on a platter with 12 slices of Parma ham, then give this simple, classic Italian *antipasto* a modern twist by scattering it with 5 torn mint leaves and drizzling over a little extra virgin olive oil.

arancini

Makes **20**
Preparation time **15 minutes**, plus making and chilling the risotto
Cooking time **1 hour**

2 tablespoons **olive oil**
1 small **carrot**, finely chopped
½ **celery stick**, finely chopped
1 **shallot**, finely chopped
150 g (5 oz) **minced beef**
250 g (8 oz) can **chopped tomatoes**
1 tablespoon **tomato purée**
1 quantity **Saffron Risotto** (see page 118), chilled overnight
75 g (3 oz) **plain flour**
2 **eggs**, beaten
250 g (8 oz) **fresh white breadcrumbs**
sunflower oil, for deep-frying

Heat the olive oil in a saucepan over a low heat. Add the carrot, celery and shallot and cook for 8–10 minutes until soft and translucent. Add the minced beef and cook, stirring and breaking up with a wooden spoon, for 5 minutes until lightly golden. Stir in the tomatoes and tomato purée. Bring to the boil, then reduce the heat and simmer very gently for about 30 minutes until the sauce becomes very thick. Leave to cool, then cover and chill for at least 1 hour.

Wet your hands, take 1 tablespoon of the cooked risotto and flatten slightly. Mould around 1 teaspoon of the meat filling to form a ball, making sure that the filling is completely encased. Repeat with the remaining risotto and filling.

Roll each arancino in the flour, then dip in the beaten egg and roll in the breadcrumbs to coat.

Heat enough sunflower oil for deep-frying in a deep saucepan to 180–190°C (350–375°F), or until a cube of bread browns in 30 seconds. Add the arancini to the hot oil, in batches, and cook for about 3–4 minutes until golden all over. Remove with a slotted spoon and drain on kitchen paper. Serve immediately.

For tomato & mozzarella arancini, follow the recipe for Saffron Risotto on page 118, but omit the saffron and replace with 6 tablespoons bought or homemade tomato sauce. Cut 125 g (4 oz) mozzarella cheese (drained weight) into bite-sized pieces. Mould the cooked, chilled risotto around the cheese pieces, then coat in breadcrumbs and deep-fry as above.

baked ricotta with bay leaves

Serves **6**
Preparation time **20 minutes**, plus soaking and chilling
Cooking time **20 minutes**

4 **sun-dried tomatoes** (dried variety)
500 g (1 lb) **ricotta cheese**
3 **large eggs**
12 **oven-dried** or **Greek-style black olives**, pitted and roughly chopped
2 tablespoons **salted capers**, rinsed and chopped
butter, for greasing
18 fresh young **bay leaves**
salt and **pepper**

To serve
olive oil
wild rocket leaves
capers

Soak the sun-dried tomatoes in a bowl of warm water for 10 minutes. Drain, pat dry and finely shred.

Push the ricotta through a sieve into a large bowl. Beat in the eggs, then lightly stir in the sun-dried tomatoes, olives and capers. Season very well with salt and pepper.

Generously grease 6 x 125 ml (4 fl oz) ramekins or ovenproof moulds. Put a bay leaf in the base of each and 2 around the side. Cover and chill to set the butter and keep the bay leaves in place.

Spoon in the ricotta mixture and level with a palette knife. Set the ramekins on a baking sheet. Bake in a preheated oven, 190°C (375°F), Gas Mark 5, for 20 minutes until set. Leave to cool, then chill.

Turn the cheeses out on to individual serving plates and serve at room temperature with a drizzle of olive oil, a few rocket leaves and some extra capers. The bay leaves should not be eaten.

For baked ricotta with rocket, Parmesan & lemon, omit the sun-dried tomatoes, olives and capers and replace with 50 g (2 oz) roughly chopped wild rocket, 3 tablespoons grated Parmesan cheese and the grated zest of 1 lemon.

salt cod pâté

Serves **4**
Preparation time **10 minutes**, plus soaking
Cooking time **15 minutes**

400 g (13 oz) **salt cod**
1 **bay leaf**
3 **garlic cloves**, peeled but kept whole
pinch of **crushed dried chillies**
milk, for poaching
75 ml (3 fl oz) **extra virgin olive oil**, plus extra for drizzling
2 tablespoons roughly chopped **flat leaf parsley**
1 **red chilli**, deseeded and finely chopped
salt (optional)
1 small **ciabatta loaf**, cut into 8 slices and griddled or toasted, to serve

Soak the salt cod in a large bowl of cold water for 48 hours, changing the water 5–6 times a day.

Drain the cod and put in a saucepan with the bay leaf, garlic and crushed chillies. Pour in enough milk to completely submerge the cod. Bring to the boil, then reduce the heat and simmer for 10 minutes. Remove the cod with a slotted spoon, reserving the poaching milk and garlic cloves, and leave until cool enough to handle. Break into flakes, removing and discarding the skin and any bones.

Process the cod with 5 tablespoons of the reserved poaching milk and the garlic cloves in a food processor until smooth. With the motor running, add the oil in a very slow, steady stream until incorporated.

Stir in the parsley, chopped fresh chilli and, if necessary, a little salt. Drizzle with oil and serve with the griddled or toasted bread.

For salt cod in batter, prepare the batter as directed on page 18. Soak and cook 500 g (1 lb) salt cod as above, then drain thoroughly and cut into 5 cm (2 inch) pieces. Heat enough sunflower oil for deep-frying in a deep saucepan to 180–190°C (350–375°F), or until a cube of bread browns in 30 seconds. Pat the salt cod pieces dry with kitchen paper, then dip in seasoned plain flour, followed by the batter. Add to the hot oil, in batches, and cook for 5–6 minutes until golden. Drain on kitchen paper. Serve with lemon wedges.

garlic cloves in olive oil

Makes **12**
Preparation time **5 minutes**
Cooking time **20 minutes**

12 large **garlic cloves**
several **rosemary sprigs**
several **thyme sprigs**
300 ml (½ pint) **olive oil**

Peel the garlic cloves and put in a small saucepan with the herb sprigs. Cover with the oil and cook over a low heat for about 20 minutes until the garlic is pale golden and soft. Leave the garlic to cool in the oil.

Transfer to a screw-top jar, pour in enough of the oil to submerge the garlic and store, covered, in the refrigerator, for up to 3 months. Use in salads, potato dishes, purées, risottos and pizzas. The flavoured oil can also be used.

For garlic in basil & chilli oil, follow the recipe as above, omitting the rosemary and thyme and replacing them with 1 whole dried red chilli. Drop 5 leaves of basil into the jar before adding the cooled garlic and oil.

mozzarella in carrozza

Serves **4**
Preparation time **10 minutes**
Cooking time **15 minutes**

3 **eggs**, lightly beaten
3 tablespoons **full-fat milk**
50 g (2 oz) **plain flour**
200 g (7 oz) **mozzarella cheese** (drained weight), cut into 5 mm (¼ inch) thick slices
8 slices of **white bread**
12 **basil leaves**
4 tablespoons **olive oil**
salt and **pepper**

Combine the eggs and milk in a bowl and season lightly with salt and pepper. Put the flour in a separate bowl.

Divide the mozzarella slices between 4 bread slices and top each with 3 basil leaves. Lay a second bread slice on top of each to make 4 sandwiches. Press down firmly on each sandwich with the heel of your hand, then cut off and discard the crusts.

Heat half the oil in a large frying pan over a medium heat. Turn 2 of the sandwiches, 1 at a time, briefly in the flour to give a light coating, then dip in the egg mixture, making sure that they are well covered. Add to the pan and cook for 3–4 minutes on each side until golden and crisp. Remove and keep warm in a low oven while you cook the second batch of sandwiches in the remaining oil. Serve with a few lettuce leaves, if liked.

For spiced Parma ham & mozzarella in carrozza, combine the eggs and milk as above, but season with salt and ¼ teaspoon chilli powder. Follow the recipe to fill the sandwiches with the mozzarella slices together with 1 slice of Parma ham for each, omitting the basil, then coat and cook as above.

proscuitto-wrapped grissini

Makes **20–25**
Preparation time **15 minutes**
Cooking time **5–8 minutes**

½ quantity **Basic Pizza Dough** (see page 15)
plain flour, for dusting
slices of **prosciutto**, cut into strips, to serve

Flavourings
coarse sea salt
sesame seeds
poppy seeds
cracked black pepper

Combine the dough balls and roll the dough out thinly on a well-floured work surface into a rectangle. Following the long side of the rectangle, cut into 5 mm (¼ inch) strips. Lightly roll each strip and taper the ends.

Brush the grissini lightly with water and sprinkle with the flavouring of your choice. Transfer to a baking sheet and bake in a preheated oven, 200°C (400°F), Gas Mark 6, for 5–8 minutes until crisp and brown. Leave to cool completely.

Twist strips of prosciutto around the grissini to serve.

For cheesy prosciutto-wrapped asparagus, cut 6 slices prosciutto in half, to give you 12 long strips. Wrap these around 12 asparagus spears and lay them on a baking sheet. Drizzle with 1 tablespoon olive oil and scatter 1 tablespoon grated Parmesan over the asparagus. Cook under a preheated grill on high, for 5–6 minutes, until the asparagus is just tender and the ham crispy.

griddled vegetable platter

Serves **4**
Preparation time **10 minutes**, plus marinating
Cooking time **20 minutes**

- 2 **courgettes**, sliced lengthways into 5 mm (¼ inch) thick slices
- 1 **aubergine**, sliced lengthways into 5 mm (¼ inch) thick slices
- 1 **yellow pepper**, cored, deseeded and cut into 2.5 cm (1 inch) wide slices
- 1 **red pepper**, cored, deseeded and cut into 2.5 cm (1 inch) wide slices
- 100 ml (3½ fl oz) **extra virgin olive oil**
- 2 **garlic cloves**, crushed
- large pinch of **crushed dried chillies**
- handful of small **mint** and/or **basil leaves**
- salt

Toss all the prepared vegetables in 2 tablespoons of the oil until well coated.

Heat a ridged griddle pan over a high heat until smoking hot. Add the courgettes and aubergine in batches and cook for 2–3 minutes on each side. Transfer to a bowl and toss with the remaining oil, the garlic and crushed chillies. Set aside.

Add the peppers in batches to the reheated griddle pan and cook for 3–4 minutes on each side, then combine with the courgettes and aubergine. Season with salt and toss in the herbs.

Cover and leave to marinate at room temperature for 30 minutes. Serve with slices of country bread.

For griddled courgettes with lemon, mint & Parmesan, omit the peppers and slice 4 large courgettes lengthways into 5 mm (¼ inch) slices, toss with oil and then griddle as above. Transfer to a bowl and toss with the remaining oil, the garlic and crushed chillies as above, adding a handful of small mint leaves, torn, but not the basil. Leave to marinate as above, then serve with a generous topping of Parmesan cheese shavings and the finely grated rind of ½ lemon.

tuna & borlotti bean salad

Serves **4**
Preparation time **15 minutes**, plus marinating
Cooking time **3 minutes**

400 g (13 oz) can **borlotti beans**, drained and rinsed
1 tablespoon **water** (optional)
2 tablespoons **extra virgin olive oil**
2 **garlic cloves**, crushed
1 **red chilli**, deseeded and finely chopped
2 **celery sticks**, thinly sliced
½ **red onion**, cut into thin wedges
200 g (7 oz) can **tuna in olive oil**, drained and flaked
finely grated **rind** and **juice** of 1 **lemon**
50 g (2 oz) **wild rocket leaves**
salt and **pepper**

Heat the borlotti beans in a saucepan over a medium heat for 3 minutes, adding the measurement water if starting to stick to the base.

Put the oil, garlic and chilli in a large bowl. Stir in the celery, onion and hot beans and season with salt and pepper. Cover and leave to marinate at room temperature for at least 30 minutes and up to 4 hours.

Stir in the tuna and lemon rind and juice. Gently toss in the rocket leaves, taste and adjust the seasoning with extra salt, pepper and lemon juice, if necessary.

For a mixed bean salad, heat the borlotti beans as above with a 400 g (13 oz) can drained and rinsed cannellini beans. Leave to marinate with the other salad ingredients as above, but also adding 2 tablespoons roughly chopped flat leaf parsley. After marinating, toss in 50 g (2 oz) lambs' lettuce, season with salt and pepper and serve.

stuffed peppers

Serves **6**
Preparation time **25 minutes**, plus steaming and marinating
Cooking time **15 minutes**

6 **red**, **orange** or **yellow peppers**
12 **artichoke hearts in olive oil**, drained
24 **anchovy fillets in olive oil**, drained
2 **garlic cloves**, sliced
1 tablespoon chopped **oregano**
extra virgin olive oil, for drizzling
2 **hard-boiled eggs**, finely chopped
salt and **pepper**

Put the whole peppers in a grill pan and cook under a preheated high grill or over a barbecue until the skins begin to char. Turn the peppers and continue to cook until charred all over.

Transfer the peppers to a plastic bag, seal and leave to steam for 10 minutes. Peel off the skins, then cut the peppers in half lengthways through the stalks and remove and discard the cores and seeds. Arrange the peppers, cut-side up, in a shallow dish.

Cut the artichokes in half and put 2 halves in each pepper half. Lay 2 anchovy fillets over the artichokes. Season well with salt and pepper. Scatter over the garlic and oregano, then drizzle with oil.

Cover and leave to marinate in the refrigerator overnight. Serve at room temperature, sprinkled with the chopped hard-boiled eggs.

For grilled peppers in herb oil, grill and peel the peppers as above. Core and deseed then cut the flesh into 2.5 cm (1 inch) strips. Roughly chop 2 rosemary sprigs and 2 thyme sprigs. Toss them into a bowl with the peppers, also adding 1 sliced garlic clove and 1 whole dried chilli. Season with salt and pour in 50 ml (2 fl oz) extra virgin olive oil. Cover and marinate in the refrigerator overnight.

seafood salad

Serves **4**
Preparation time **20 minutes**, plus chilling
Cooking time **10 minutes**

500 g (1 lb) **mussels**, cleaned (see page 14)
300 g (10 oz) **clams**, cleaned (see page 14)
1 **onion**, quartered
1 **bay leaf**
300 g (10 oz) **small squid**, cleaned (see page 14) and cut into 2.5 cm (1 inch) rounds
300 g (10 oz) **raw peeled king prawns**
8 small **shelled scallops**, with or without roe
juice of 2 **lemons**
2 **garlic cloves**, finely chopped
4 tablespoons **olive oil**
2 **celery sticks**, thinly sliced
1 **carrot**, cut into small cubes
1 **red pepper**, cored, deseeded and cut into small cubes
3 **spring onions**, thinly sliced
salt and **pepper**
crusty bread, to serve

Put the shellfish and 100 ml (3½ fl oz) water in a large saucepan with a tight-fitting lid. Cover and bring to the boil over a high heat. Cook, shaking the pan frequently, for 4–5 minutes, or until the shells have opened. Remove with a slotted spoon, discarding any that remain closed. Remove the flesh from the shells and put in a large bowl.

Return the pan with the cooking liquid to a high heat, add 400 ml (14 fl oz) water, the onion and bay leaf and bring to the boil. Add the seafood and cook for 2–3 minutes until the prawns turn pink and the scallops are opaque all the way though. Remove with a slotted spoon and add to the shellfish.

Boil the liquid until reduced to 50 ml (2 fl oz). Remove from the heat and stir in the lemon juice, garlic and oil. Season with salt and pepper, pour over the seafood and shellfish and toss well.

Leave to cool to room temperature, then toss in the remaining ingredients. Cover and chill for at least 30 minutes and up to 24 hours. Serve the salad with crusty bread.

For seafood rice salad, cook the shellfish, then the seafood as above. Remove from the pan, discard the onion and bay leaf and stir in a large pinch of saffron threads. Boil rapidly until reduced to 100 ml (3½ fl oz). Toss in 200 g (7 oz) freshly cooked long-grain rice. Remove from the heat and stir well. Add the seafood and remaining ingredients as above, but omit the red pepper.

crudités & garlic anchovy dip

Serves **4–6**
Preparation time **10 minutes**
Cooking time **15 minutes**

50 ml (2 fl oz) **milk**
6 **garlic cloves**, peeled but kept whole
150 g (5 oz) **anchovy fillets in olive oil**, drained and roughly chopped
75 g (3 oz) **butter**
75 ml (3 fl oz) **extra virgin olive oil**

Crudités
8 **baby carrots**, peeled
250 g (8 oz) **cauliflower florets**
4 **celery sticks**, cut in half
½ **red cabbage**, cut into thin wedges
5 **baby fennel**, cut in half lengthways

Put the milk, garlic and anchovies in a small saucepan over a low heat and cook gently for 15 minutes, without letting the milk come to the boil, until the anchovies have melted into the pan and the garlic is soft.

Use the back of a fork to mash the garlic against the side of the pan. Add the butter and oil and stir until the butter has melted. Transfer to a small serving bowl.

Arrange the crudités in a large serving dish, leaving space for the bowl of sauce, and serve while the sauce is still warm for dipping.

For garlic & caper mayonnaise, to serve in place of the garlic anchovy dip, put 2 egg yolks and 1 crushed garlic clove in a food processor. With the motor running, add 250 ml (8 fl oz) olive oil in a very slow, steady stream until incorporated, then stir in 1½ tablespoons roughly chopped, rinsed capers in brine. Season with salt and pepper and serve with the crudités as above.

pasta & pizza

orecchiette with broccoli

Serves **4**
Preparation time **10 minutes**
Cooking time **15 minutes**

500 g (1 lb) **broccoli**, roughly chopped
400 g (13 oz) **dried orecchiette**
5 tablespoons **extra virgin olive oil**
2 **anchovy fillets in olive oil**, drained and roughly chopped
large pinch of **crushed dried chillies**
2 **garlic cloves**, sliced
4 tablespoons freshly grated **Parmesan cheese**, plus extra to serve

Bring a large saucepan of salted water to the boil and tip in the broccoli and pasta. Cook for about 14 minutes, or according to the pasta packet instructions, until the pasta is al dente and the broccoli is cooked and starting to fall apart.

Meanwhile, pour the oil into a large frying pan and add the anchovies, crushed chillies and garlic and heat over a very low heat for 5–6 minutes until the anchovies have melted into the oil.

Drain the pasta, reserving a ladleful of the cooking water, and toss the pasta and broccoli into the pan with the anchovy oil. Toss over a high heat for 30 seconds, then pour in the reserved cooking water and continue stirring over the heat for a further 30 seconds. Work the Parmesan into the pasta, then serve with an extra scattering of Parmesan.

For penne with creamy cauliflower, follow the recipe as above, but replace the broccoli with 500 g (1 lb) roughly chopped cauliflower and the orecchiette with 400 g (13 oz) dried penne. Instead of adding the reserved cooking water to the pan at the end of the recipe, stir in 250 g (8 oz) crème fraîche with the Parmesan.

wild mushroom lasagne

Serves **6**
Preparation time **20 minutes**, plus cooling
Cooking time **45 minutes**

100 g (3½ oz) **unsalted butter**, plus extra for greasing
4 tablespoons **plain flour**
1 litre (1¾ pints) **milk**
large pinch of freshly grated **nutmeg**
3 tablespoons roughly chopped **flat leaf parsley**
5 tablespoons freshly grated **Parmesan cheese**
1 tablespoon **olive oil**
625 g (1¼ lb) **mixed wild mushrooms**, trimmed and thickly sliced
1 **garlic clove**, crushed
100 ml (3½ fl oz) **dry white wine**
25 g (1 oz) **dried porcini mushrooms**, soaked in 100 ml (3½ fl oz) hot water for 10 minutes
300 g (10 oz) **fresh lasagne sheets**
truffle oil, for drizzling
salt and **pepper**

Melt half the butter in a saucepan over a low heat. Add the flour and cook, stirring with a wooden spoon, for 1–2 minutes until a pale biscuity colour. Remove from the heat and gradually stir in the milk until smooth. Return to a medium heat and cook, stirring constantly, until thick and velvety. Add the nutmeg and season with salt and pepper, then stir in the parsley and 2 tablespoons of the Parmesan. Remove from the heat and leave to cool to room temperature.

Melt the remaining butter with the oil in a large, heavy-based frying pan. Add the fresh mushrooms and cook over a high heat for 2 minutes. Stir in the garlic and cook for 1 minute. Season with salt and pepper. Pour in the wine and porcini and their soaking water. Cook, stirring, until the liquid has evaporated. Stir into the white sauce.

Grease an ovenproof dish, about 19 x 30 cm (8 x 12 inches). Cover the base with a layer of slightly overlapping lasagne sheets. Top with a quarter of the sauce, then continue layering, finishing with a layer of sauce. Scatter with the remaining Parmesan. Bake in a preheated oven, 200°C (400°F), Gas Mark 6, for 30 minutes. Drizzle lightly with truffle oil and serve with a green salad, if liked.

For mushroom, blue cheese & spinach lasagne,

follow the recipe above, but stir 75 g (3 oz) chopped gorgonzola and 100 g (3½ oz) baby spinach into the white sauce instead of the parsley in the first step, then omit the dried porcini.

fusilli with tuna, capers & mint

Serves **4**
Preparation time **10 minutes**
Cooking time **12 minutes**

300 g (10 oz) canned **tuna in olive oil**
4 tablespoons **extra virgin olive oil**, plus extra for drizzling
finely grated **rind** of 1 **lemon**
2 **garlic cloves**, crushed
2 tablespoons **capers in brine**, drained and rinsed
½ **red chilli**, deseeded and finely chopped
2 tablespoons roughly chopped **mint**
400 g (13 oz) **dried fusilli**
salt

Put the tuna with its oil in a large serving bowl. Break it up with a fork, then stir in the remaining ingredients, except for the pasta. Season with salt. Cover and leave to infuse while you cook the pasta.

Cook the pasta in a large saucepan of salted boiling water for about 10–12 minutes, or according to the packet instructions, until al dente.

Drain the pasta and toss into the sauce. Serve immediately with a bottle of extra virgin olive oil for anyone to drizzle a little extra over their serving.

For penne with grilled vegetables, capers & mint, replace the tuna with 300 g (10 oz) mixed bottled grilled vegetables in olive oil, such as peppers, courgettes and aubergines. Drain the vegetables, reserving the oil from the jars. Roughly chop and put in a bowl with 4 tablespoons of the reserved oil and the remaining ingredients as above. Season with salt. Cover and leave to infuse while you cook 400 g (13 oz) dried penne, instead of the fusilli, as above. Drain and toss with the sauce.

spaghetti with clams & chilli

Serves **4**
Preparation time **10 minutes**
Cooking time **20 minutes**

5 tablespoons **extra virgin olive oil**
2 **garlic cloves**, thinly sliced
¼ teaspoon **crushed dried chillies**
400 g (13 oz) **dried spaghetti**
150 ml (¼ pint) **dry white wine**
1 kg (2 lb) **clams**, cleaned (see page 14)
2 tablespoons roughly chopped **flat leaf parsley**

Heat the oil in the largest frying pan you have or a wok over a low heat. Add the garlic and crushed chillies and leave to infuse for 6–8 minutes. If the garlic begins to colour, remove the pan from the heat and leave to infuse in the heat of the pan.

Cook the pasta in a large saucepan of salted boiling water for 8–10 minutes, or according to the packet instructions, until al dente, then drain.

Meanwhile, increase the heat under the frying pan and pour in the wine. Boil for 1 minute, then add the clams and cook, stirring, for 4–5 minutes until the shells have opened. Stir in the drained pasta and the parsley and toss over a high heat for 30 seconds. Serve immediately.

For spaghetti with clams, pancetta & tomatoes, heat the oil in a large frying pan or wok as above. Add 75 g (3 oz) cubed pancetta and cook for 3–4 minutes until golden and crisp. Add the garlic and leave to infuse over a low heat for 10 minutes. Cook the pasta as above. Add the wine to the frying pan and boil for 1 minute as above, then add the clams with 100 g (3½ oz) halved cherry tomatoes and complete the recipe as above.

rocket & tomato tagliatelle

Serves **4**
Preparation time **10 minutes**
Cooking time **8–12 minutes**

500 g (1 lb) **dried tagliatelle**
3 tablespoons **olive oil**
2 **garlic cloves**, finely chopped
500 g (1 lb) **very ripe cherry tomatoes**, halved
1 tablespoon **balsamic vinegar**
175 g (6 oz) **wild rocket leaves**
salt and **pepper**
Parmesan cheese shavings, to serve

Cook the pasta in a large saucepan of salted boiling water for 8–12 minutes, or according to packet instructions, until al dente, then drain.

Meanwhile, heat the oil in a frying pan, add the garlic and cook, stirring, for 1 minute until golden. Add the tomatoes and cook for barely 1 minute, or until just heated through and beginning to disintegrate.

Sprinkle the tomatoes with the vinegar and allow to evaporate. Toss in the rocket and carefully stir to mix with the tomatoes. Heat through until the rocket is just wilted. Season well with salt and pepper.

Toss the rocket and tomato mixture with the hot cooked pasta and serve immediately, scattered with plenty of Parmesan shavings.

For tomato & pancetta tagliatelle, replace the dried tagliatelle with 500 g (1 lb) egg tagliatelle. Heat the oil in a frying pan with 100 g (3½ oz) cubed pancetta. Fry for 4–5 minutes, over a medium heat, until golden then stir in the garlic and cook for 1 minute. Add the tomatoes and complete the recipe as above, omitting the balsamic vinegar and rocket.

roasted tomato & pancetta pasta

Serves **4**
Preparation time **5 minutes**
Cooking time **about 1 hour**

500 g (1 lb) **cherry tomatoes**
3 tablespoons **olive oil**
400 g (13 oz) **dried rigatoni** or **penne**
100 g (3½ oz) **pancetta**, cubed
1 **garlic clove**, thinly sliced
2 **shallots**, thinly sliced
large pinch of **crushed dried chillies**
aged balsamic vinegar, for drizzling
salt

Put the whole tomatoes in a large roasting tin and drizzle with 2 tablespoons of the oil. Slow-roast in a preheated oven, 150°C (300°F), Gas Mark 2, for 1 hour, or until they look semi-dried.

Meanwhile, cook the pasta in a large saucepan of salted boiling water for about 10–12 minutes, or according to the packet instructions, until al dente.

While the pasta is cooking, heat the remaining oil in a large frying pan. Add the pancetta, garlic, shallots and crushed chillies and cook over a low heat for 10 minutes, or until the shallots are golden and the pancetta nice and crispy.

Toss the roasted tomatoes into the frying pan, reserving a few for garnishing. Drain the pasta, reserving a ladleful of the cooking water. Add the pasta to the sauce and toss over a high heat for a few seconds. Add the reserved cooking water and continue tossing for another 30 seconds. Serve immediately, garnished with the reserved roasted tomatoes and a drizzle of aged balsamic vinegar.

For roasted tomato, pancetta & spinach salad, slow-roast the tomatoes and cook the pancetta with the garlic, shallots and crushed chillies as above. Toss all these ingredients into 75 g (3 oz) baby spinach in a salad bowl. Whisk together 2 tablespoons extra virgin olive oil, 2 teaspoons aged balsamic vinegar and salt to taste in a small bowl, add to the salad and toss to coat. Shave over some Parmesan cheese to serve.

fettuccine & dried porcini sauce

Serves **4**
Preparation time **10 minutes**, plus soaking
Cooking time **20 minutes**

25 g (1 oz) **dried porcini mushrooms**, soaked in 200 ml (7 fl oz) hot water for 10 minutes
2 tablespoons **olive oil**
2 **garlic cloves**, finely chopped
2 tablespoons roughly chopped **thyme**
500 ml (17 fl oz) **chicken** or **vegetable stock**
200 ml (7 fl oz) **full-bodied red wine**
400 g (13 oz) **dried fettuccine**
40 g (1½ oz) **unsalted butter**, cubed
salt and **pepper**
freshly grated **Parmesan cheese**, to serve

Drain the porcini, reserving the soaking water, and squeeze out any excess moisture.

Heat the oil in a heavy-based frying pan over a medium heat. Add the garlic and thyme and cook, stirring, for 30 seconds. Increase the heat to high. Add the porcini, season with salt and pepper and cook, stirring, for 1 minute. Pour in the reserved soaking water, stock and wine. Bring to the boil, then simmer, uncovered, over a very low heat for 15 minutes. Taste and adjust the seasoning.

Meanwhile, cook the pasta in a large saucepan of salted boiling water for 8–10 minutes, or according to the packet instructions, until al dente. Drain thoroughly, reserving a ladleful of the cooking water.

Return the pasta to the pan and place over a low heat. Stir in the sauce and the butter and combine thoroughly. Add the reserved cooking water and cook, stirring, for a few seconds until the pasta is well coated and looks silky. Serve immediately with grated Parmesan.

For fettuccine with creamy mushroom & tarragon sauce, heat the oil as above, add 300 g (10 oz) sliced chestnut mushrooms and 2 finely chopped garlic cloves and cook, stirring, for 5 minutes. Add the stock and 100 ml (3½ fl oz) dry white wine, instead of the red, and bring to the boil. Reduce the heat and simmer as above, adding 150 g (5 oz) crème fraîche and 2 tablespoons chopped tarragon for the last 5 minutes of cooking. Combine with the cooked drained fettuccine, as above, and serve immediately.

lemon, rocket & basil linguine

Serves **4**
Preparation time **10 minutes**
Cooking time **about 10 minutes**

400 g (13 oz) **dried linguine**
50 g (2 oz) **unsalted butter**
finely grated **rind** and **juice** of 1 **lemon**
6 **basil leaves**, torn
100 g (3½ oz) **wild rocket leaves**
50 g (2 oz) **Parmesan cheese**, freshly grated
salt and **pepper**

Cook the pasta in a large saucepan of salted boiling water for 8–10 minutes, or according to packet instructions, until al dente.

Drain the pasta, reserving half a ladleful of the cooking water. Return the pasta to the pan and place over a low heat. Add all the remaining ingredients, season generously with pepper and stir until the butter has melted and the pasta is evenly coated. If it looks slightly dry, add some of the reserved cooking water. Serve immediately.

For tortellini with lemon, pea & basil sauce, instead of the linguine, cook 500 g (1 lb) fresh spinach and ricotta tortellini in a large saucepan of salted boiling water according to the packet instructions until al dente. Meanwhile, put the butter, lemon rind and juice, basil, rocket and Parmesan as above in a food processor with 150 g (5 oz) peas, thawed if frozen. Pulse to a coarse paste. Drain the tortellini and return to the pan. Add the sauce, toss with the tortellini and serve immediately.

meatballs with spaghetti

Serves **4**
Preparation time **20 minutes**
Cooking time **1 hour 20 minutes**

2 slices of **stale bread**, crusts removed
75 ml (3 fl oz) **milk**
4 tablespoons **olive oil**
6 **spring onions** or 1 small **onion**, chopped
1 **garlic clove**, chopped
750 g (1½ lb) **lean minced beef**
2 tablespoons freshly grated **Parmesan cheese**
freshly grated **nutmeg**
300 ml (½ pint) **dry white wine**
400 g (13 oz) can **chopped tomatoes**
2 **bay leaves**
salt and **pepper**
freshly cooked **spaghetti**, to serve
basil leaves, to garnish

Put the bread in a large bowl, moisten with the milk and leave to soak.

Heat half the oil in a frying pan over a medium heat. Add the spring onions or onion and garlic and cook for 5 minutes until soft and just beginning to brown.

Combine the minced beef with the moistened bread, the cooked onions and garlic and Parmesan, and season with nutmeg, salt and pepper. Work together with your hands until the mixture is well mixed and smooth. With clean, wet hands, roll the mixture into 28 even-sized balls.

Heat the remaining oil in a large, nonstick frying pan. Add the meatballs, in batches, and cook until browned all over. Transfer to a shallow ovenproof dish.

Add the wine and tomatoes to the pan and bring to the boil, scraping up any sediment from the base. Add the bay leaves, season with salt and pepper and boil rapidly for 5 minutes. Pour over the meatballs, cover with foil and bake in a preheated oven, 180°C (350°F), Gas Mark 4, for 1 hour, or until tender. Serve with spaghetti, garnished with basil leaves.

For pork meatballs in a tomato & red pepper sauce, replace the beef mince with 750 g (1½ lb) pork mince. Shape and brown as above and place in an ovenproof dish with 125 g (4 oz) bought roasted peppers, cut into 2.5 cm (1 inch) pieces. Complete the recipe as above.

spinach potato gnocchi

Serves **4–6**
Preparation time **30 minutes**, plus resting
Cooking time **25 minutes**

1 kg (2 lb) **floury potatoes**, such as King Edwards or Maris Piper, unpeeled
¼ **whole nutmeg**, freshly grated
150–300 g (5–10 oz) **plain flour**, plus extra for dusting
50 g (2 oz) **baby spinach**, finely chopped
2 **eggs**
salt and **pepper**

Lemon sage butter
50 g (2 oz) **butter**
6 whole **sage leaves**
finely grated **rind** of 1 **lemon**

Put the potatoes in a saucepan and cover with water. Cover the pan and bring to the boil. Reduce the heat and simmer for about 20 minutes until cooked through – a potato pierced with a blunt knife should slide off the blade. Drain and leave until cool enough to handle.

Peel the warm potatoes, then pass through a mouli or ricer to make a light, smooth mash. Transfer to a large bowl, add the nutmeg and season with salt and pepper. Sift in 150 g (5 oz) flour and add the spinach. Break in the eggs, then gently but quickly work the mixture through your fingers until it reaches a lumpy breadcrumb consistency. Tip the mixture on to a work surface and gently knead to a soft, smooth and pliable dough, adding more flour if too wet. Be careful not to overwork, or the gnocchi will lose their light quality.

Divide the dough into 3 pieces and roll each piece into a finger-thick length. Using a sharp knife, cut into 2.5 cm (1 inch) pieces. Transfer to a floured tray and leave to rest for 10–20 minutes. Meanwhile heat the butter ingredients in a frying pan, until the butter has melted and leave to infuse.

Bring a large saucepan of salted water to the boil. Add the gnocchi, return to the boil and cook for 3–4 minutes, or until they float to the surface. Remove with a slotted spoon into a frying pan with the melted butter. Toss well and serve immediately.

For rocket gnocchi, replace the spinach with 50 g (2 oz) wild rocket, finely chopped. Add the rind of 1 lemon to the potatoes. Complete as above, replacing the sage leaves with 2 tablespoons chopped parsley.

spaghetti with charred asparagus

Serves **4**
Preparation time **10 minutes**
Cooking time **15 minutes**

500 g (1 lb) **thin asparagus spears**, trimmed
3–4 tablespoons **extra virgin olive oil**
juice of 1 **lemon**
375 g (12 oz) **dried spaghetti**
2 **garlic cloves**, roughly chopped
¼–½ teaspoon **dried chilli flakes**
25 g (1 oz) **basil leaves**
25 g (1 oz) freshly grated **Parmesan cheese**, plus extra to serve (optional)
salt and **pepper**

Brush the asparagus spears with a little of the oil. Cook in a preheated ridged griddle pan or under a preheated high grill, turning once, until charred and tender. Toss with a little more of the oil, half the lemon juice and salt and pepper. Set aside.

Cook the pasta in a large saucepan of salted boiling water for 8–10 minutes, or according to the packet instructions, until al dente.

Just before the pasta is cooked, heat the remaining oil in a large frying pan or wok over a medium heat. Add the garlic with a little salt and cook, stirring, for 3–4 minutes until softened but not browned. Add the chilli flakes and asparagus and heat through.

Drain the pasta, reserving a ladleful of the cooking water, and add both to the frying pan with the basil, remaining lemon juice, the Parmesan and pepper to taste. Serve immediately, with extra Parmesan, if liked.

For pasta salad with mozzarella & asparagus, complete the first step of the recipe as above and toss into 400 g (13 oz) freshly cooked penne. Toss in the remaining ingredients and leave to marinate while the pasta and asparagus cool to room temperature. Roughly chop 200 g (7 oz) mozzarella and toss into the pasta, adding extra olive oil, if needed.

onion, gorgonzola & walnut pizza

Serves **4**
Preparation time **10 minutes**, plus making the pizza dough
Cooking time **40–45 minutes**

1 quantity **Basic Pizza Dough** (see page 15)
a little dressed **rocket**, to garnish (optional)

Topping
3 **red onions**
2 tablespoons **extra virgin olive oil**, plus extra to drizzle
2 tablespoons chopped **sage**
1 tablespoon **balsamic vinegar**
175 g (6 oz) **Gorgonzola cheese**, crumbled
4 tablespoons **crème fraîche**
45 g (1½ oz) shelled **walnuts**, roughly chopped
pepper

Prepare the topping while the pizza dough is rising. Cut each onion into eight wedges, place them in a shallow roasting dish and drizzle over the oil. Top with half of the sage and season well with salt and pepper. Roast in a preheated oven, 220°C (425°F), Gas Mark 7, for 25–30 minutes until soft and caramelized. Add the vinegar and cook for a further 5 minutes. Leave to cool.

Increase the oven temperature to 240°C (475°F), Gas Mark 9 and place a large baking sheet on the middle shelf. Cream together the Gorgonzola and crème fraîche.

Roll out one piece of pizza dough on a floured surface to form a thin 23 cm (9 inch) round. Transfer to a well floured board or second baking sheet and top with a quarter each of the onions, the cheese mixture, the remaining sage and walnuts. Season with pepper and drizzle with a little olive oil.

Slide the pizza on to the heated baking sheet. Bake for 10–12 minutes until the base is crisp and the topping melted. Prepare the second pizza while the first one is cooking and so on with all four.

Serve the pizzas garnished with a little rocket, if liked.

For potato & cheese pizza, peel and thinly slice 3 medium potatoes and roast for 20 minutes with sage and oil, in place of the onions, as above. Use to top the pizza with the creamed cheese and walnuts, as above, adding a scattering of grated Parmesan, before baking. Omit the vinegar.

pizza fiorentina

Serves **4**
Preparation time **10 minutes**, plus making the pizza dough
Cooking time **35 minutes**

1 tablespoon **olive oil**, plus extra for drizzling and glazing
2 **garlic cloves**, crushed
500 g (1 lb) **baby spinach**
1 quantity **Basic Pizza Dough** (see page 15)
plain flour, for dusting
200 ml (7 fl oz) **passata**
200 g (7 oz) **mozzarella cheese** (drained weight), chopped
20 **black olives**
4 **eggs**
salt and **pepper**

Heat the oil in a large frying pan with the garlic for 15 seconds, then add the spinach and cook over a high heat for 1–2 minutes until just wilted. Season lightly with salt and pepper.

Heat a baking sheet in a preheated oven, 240°C (475°F), Gas Mark 9. Place 1 pizza dough ball on the base only of a well-floured, 23 cm (9 inch) loose-bottomed tart tin. Push down on the dough with your fingertips, pressing it out to fill the base, leaving the border slightly thicker. If you get any tears, forcefully pinch the dough around the hole back together.

Spoon 3 tablespoons of the passata over the base and scatter with a quarter of the mozzarella, spinach and olives. Crack 1 egg on to the pizza, drizzle with oil and season lightly with salt and pepper. Brush the border with oil to glaze. Remove the baking sheet from the oven, slide the tin on to it, then quickly return to the oven. Bake for 7–8 minutes until crisp and risen. Serve immediately. As the first pizza cooks, prepare the next for the oven.

For spinach, anchovy & caper pizza, cook the spinach and prepare the pizza base as above. Brush with olive oil, then top with a quarter of the mozzarella and spinach, as above, omitting the olives and egg. Arrange 5 drained anchovy fillets in olive oil over the pizza and scatter with 1 teaspoon rinsed capers in brine. Drizzle with chilli oil and cook as above. Repeat to make 3 more pizzas.

prosciutto & artichoke sfincione

Serves **4**
Preparation time **30 minutes**, plus rising
Cooking time **15–20 minutes**

- 15 g (½ oz) **fresh yeast** or ½ tablespoon **fast-action dried yeast**
- pinch of **caster sugar**
- 250 ml (8 fl oz) **lukewarm water**
- 375 g (12 oz) **plain flour**, plus extra for dusting
- 2 tablespoons **olive oil**, plus extra for oiling and drizzling
- ½ teaspoon **salt**
- 3 tablespoons **sun-dried tomato purée**
- 1 **mozzarella cheese**, weighing about 150 g (5 oz) (drained weight), thinly sliced
- 4 **ripe plum tomatoes**, cut into long wedges
- 8 **artichoke hearts in olive oil**, drained and halved
- 4 large **garlic cloves**, sliced
- 6 slices **prosciutto**
- 3 tablespoons freshly grated **Parmesan cheese**
- **basil leaves**, to garnish

Cream the fresh yeast with the sugar in a bowl, then whisk in the water. For dried yeast, dissolve the yeast in a bowl with the sugar, water and 2 tablespoons of the flour. Cover with a moist cloth and leave to stand in a warm place for 10 minutes until foamy.

Sift the flour into a large bowl and make a well in the centre. Add the yeast mixture, oil and salt to the well and mix with a round-bladed knife, then with your hands, until the dough comes together. Knead on a floured work surface for about 10 minutes until smooth and elastic. It should be quite soft, but if it is too soft to handle, add a little more flour. Put in an oiled bowl, cover with a moist cloth and leave to rise in a warm place for 1 hour, or until doubled in size.

Knock the dough back and roll out to a 30 cm (12 inch) circle, leaving the border slightly thicker. Slide on to a large floured baking sheet.

Spread the tomato purée over the pizza base. Arrange half the mozzarella on top. Scatter over the tomatoes, artichokes and garlic. Drape the prosciutto over the pizza. Scatter over the Parmesan and remaining mozzarella. Drizzle with oil and bake in a preheated oven, 240°C, (475°F), Gas Mark 9, for 15–20 minutes until golden. Serve garnished with basil leaves.

For tomato, onion and anchovy sfincione, prepare the dough as above. For the topping, cook 1 large sliced onion in 2 tablespoons olive oil. Add 300 ml (½ pint) passata, 1 crushed garlic clove and 8 chopped anchovy fillets. Scatter with 150 g (5 oz) chopped mozzarella and bake as above.

pizza with speck & dolcelatte

Serves **4**
Preparation time **15 minutes**, plus making the pizza dough
Cooking time **35 minutes**

200 ml (7 fl oz) **passata**
5 large **basil leaves**, torn, plus extra to garnish
1 **garlic clove**, crushed
1 tablespoon **extra virgin olive oil**, plus extra for glazing
1 quantity **Basic Pizza Dough** (see page 15)
plain flour, for dusting
125 g (4 oz) **mozzarella cheese** (drained weight), torn into chunks
12 slices of **speck**
75 g (3 oz) **dolcelatte cheese**, broken into pieces
salt

Combine the passata, basil, garlic and oil in a bowl. Season with salt, cover and leave to infuse for 15 minutes.

Heat a baking sheet in a preheated oven, 240°C (475°F), Gas Mark 9. Place 1 pizza dough ball on the base only of a well-floured, 23 cm (9 inch) loose-bottomed tart tin. Push down on the dough with your fingertips, pressing it out to fill the base, leaving the border slightly thicker. If you get any tears, forcefully pinch the dough around the hole back together.

Spoon 3 tablespoons of the passata mix over the base and scatter with a quarter of the mozzarella. Brush the border with oil to glaze. Remove the heated baking sheet from the oven, slide the tin on to it, then quickly return to the oven. Bake for 7–8 minutes until crisp and risen. Top with 3 slices of speck, then half the dolcelatte. Serve immediately, garnished with a little torn basil. As the first pizza cooks, prepare the next for the oven.

For pizza with smoked mozzarella, Parma ham & rocket, prepare the passata mixture and pizza base as above. Top the tomato mixture with 125 g (4 oz) smoked mozzarella slices, divided between the 4 pizza bases. Bake as above, then top each pizza with 3 slices of Parma ham and 15 g (½ oz) wild rocket leaves.

aubergine, basil & ricotta pizza

Serves **4**
Preparation time **10 minutes**, plus making the pizza dough
Cooking time **50 minutes**

150 ml (¼ pint) **passata**
5 large **basil leaves**, torn
1 **garlic clove**, crushed
2–3 small–medium **aubergines**, sliced lengthways into 5 mm (¼ inch) thick slices
1 quantity **Basic Pizza Dough** (see page 15)
plain flour, for dusting
125 g (4 oz) **ricotta cheese**, broken into small chunks
75 g (3 oz) **mozzarella cheese** (drained weight), roughly chopped
olive oil, for glazing
salt
basil leaves, to garnish

Combine the passata, basil and garlic in a bowl. Season lightly with salt, cover and leave to infuse while you cook the aubergines.

Heat a ridged griddle pan over a high heat until smoking hot. Add the aubergine, in batches, and cook for 2 minutes on each side until charred on the outside and soft all the way through.

Heat a baking sheet in a preheated oven, 240°C (475°F), Gas Mark 9. Place 1 pizza dough ball on the base only of a well-floured, 23 cm (9 inch) loose-bottomed tart tin. Push down on the dough with your fingertips, pressing it out to fill the base, leaving the border slightly thicker. If you get any tears, forcefully pinch the dough around the hole back together.

Spoon 2 tablespoons of the passata mixture over the base, top with a quarter of the aubergines, then scatter with a quarter each of the cheeses. Brush the border with oil, to glaze. Remove the heated baking sheet from the oven, slide the tin on to it, then quickly return to the oven. Bake for 7–8 minutes until crisp and risen. Serve immediately, garnished with basil leaves. As the first pizza cooks, prepare the next for the oven.

For courgette & smoked mozzarella pizza, replace the aubergines with 4 courgettes and griddle as above. Omit the ricotta and mozzarella and replace with 150 g (5 oz) sliced smoked mozzarella.

olive, onion & rosemary focaccia

Serves **6**
Preparation time **2 hours, 20 minutes**
Cooking time **about 20 minutes**

15 g (½ oz) **fresh yeast** or 1½ teaspoons **fast-action dried yeast**
large pinch **caster sugar**
225 ml (7½ fl oz) **lukewarm water**
350 g (11½ oz) **Italian '00' flour** or **plain flour**, plus extra for dusting
½ teaspoon **salt**
olive oil, for oiling and drizzling
1 **onion**, thinly sliced
50 g (2 oz) **pitted black olives**
3 **rosemary sprigs**, leaves only
coarse sea salt, for sprinkling

Dissolve the yeast in a bowl with the sugar, water and half the flour. Cover with a moist cloth and leave to stand in a warm place for 15 minutes until foamy.

Stir the salt into the remaining flour, then tip into the yeast mixture. Stir with one hand to form a moist dough. Knead on a floured work surface for 10 minutes until smooth and elastic. It should be very soft and slightly sticky. If too sticky to handle, add a little more flour. Put in an oiled bowl, cover with a moist cloth and leave to rise in a warm place for 1 hour, or until doubled in size.

Gently knead half the onion and olives into the dough. Transfer to a lightly oiled rectangular baking tray, about 20 x 30 cm (8 x 12 inches), stretching it to fill the tray. Cover with a moist cloth and leave to rise in a warm place for 30 minutes. Make deep dimples on the surface with your finger. Scatter with the rosemary and remaining onion and olives and drizzle with oil. Cover again and leave to rise for 15 minutes.

Sprinkle the top of the focaccia with coarse sea salt. Bake in a preheated oven, 200°C (400°F), Gas Mark 6, for 20 minutes. The bread is ready when the base sounds hollow when tapped. If not, bake for a further 5 minutes. Turn out on to a wire rack and leave to cool. Eat warm or at room temperature on the same day.

For basil & tomato focaccia, follow the recipe up to the end of the second step. Knead 5 tablespoons chopped basil into the dough, then transfer to the baking tray and leave to rise for 30 minutes. Make dimples in the surface, scatter with 15 whole cherry tomatoes and leave to rise for 15 minutes. Season and bake as above.

cherry tomato & rocket pizza

Serves **4**
Preparation time **15 minutes**, plus making the pizza dough
Cooking time **35 minutes**

200 g (7 oz) **cherry tomatoes**
2 **garlic cloves**, crushed
large pinch of **crushed dried chillies**
2 tablespoons **olive oil**, plus extra for glazing
1 quantity **Basic Pizza Dough** (see page 15)
plain flour, for dusting
150 g (5 oz) **buffalo mozzarella cheese**, drained and torn into large pieces
50 g (2 oz) **wild rocket leaves**
salt

Put the tomatoes in a large bowl and crush them between your fingers. Add the garlic and crushed chillies, then stir in half the oil. Season with salt, cover and leave to infuse.

Heat a baking sheet in a preheated oven, 240°C (475°F), Gas Mark 9. Place 1 pizza dough ball on the base only of a well-floured, 23 cm (9 inch) loose-bottomed tart tin. Push down on the dough with your fingertips, pressing it out to fill the base, leaving the border slightly thicker. If you get any tears, forcefully pinch the dough around the hole back together.

Spoon a quarter of the tomato mixture over the base, then brush the border with oil to glaze. Remove the heated baking sheet from the oven, slide the tin on to it, then quickly return to the oven. Bake for 7–8 minutes until crisp and risen. Scatter with a quarter each of the mozzarella and rocket and serve immediately. As the first pizza cooks, prepare the next for the oven.

For mozzarella & rocket pizza rolls, roll out the whole dough quantity into a rectangle, approximately 1 cm (½ inch) thick. Finely chop the mozzarella and rocket and scatter over the dough with the garlic, chilli and olive oil. Roll up the dough, like a Swiss roll, and cut into 2.5 cm (1 inch) pieces. Lay the rolls on an oiled baking sheet and bake for 12–15 minutes. Omit the cherry tomatoes.

soups, rice & polenta

barley, bean & porcini soup

Serves **4**
Preparation time **10 minutes**, plus soaking
Cooking time **1 hour 35 minutes**

100 g (3½ oz) **dried borlotti beans**
100 g (3½ oz) **dried cannellini beans**
2 litres (3½ pints) **vegetable** or **chicken stock**
2 **celery sticks**, cubed
1 large **carrot**, cubed
1 **onion**, cubed
1 **bay leaf**
¼ teaspoon **crushed dried chillies**
75 g (3 oz) **pearl barley**
20 g (¾ oz) **dried porcini mushrooms**
2 tablespoons roughly chopped **flat leaf parsley**
salt and **pepper**

To serve
freshly grated **Parmesan cheese**
extra virgin olive oil

Put the dried beans in a large bowl, cover with cold water and leave to soak overnight.

Drain the soaked beans, put in a large saucepan and cover with the stock. Stir in the vegetables, bay leaf and crushed chillies and bring to the boil. Reduce the heat and skim off any scum that has risen to the surface. Simmer, uncovered, for 1 hour.

Stir the pearl barley and porcini into the pan and quickly return to the boil. Skim off any scum, reduce the heat and simmer for a further 30 minutes, or until the beans and barley are very tender.

Add the parsley, then check the seasoning, adding salt and pepper to taste. Serve with a scattering of grated Parmesan and a light drizzle of extra virgin olive oil.

For borlotti, pasta & red mullet soup, soak 200 g (7 oz) dried borlotti beans in cold water overnight, then cook with the stock, vegetables, bay leaves and crushed chillies, as in the second step above, increasing the cooking time to 1½ hours. Increase the heat to a rapid boil and stir in 150 g (5 oz) dried small pasta shapes. Cook for 6 minutes, then add 250 g (8 oz) red mullet fillets, cut into 3.5 cm (1½ inch) pieces. Cook for a further 2 minutes, or until the pasta is al dente. Scatter with 2 tablespoons roughly chopped flat leaf parsley and drizzle with extra virgin olive oil to serve.

chestnut, rice & pancetta soup

Serves **4**
Preparation time **10 minutes**
Cooking time **35 minutes**

50 g (2 oz) **butter**
150 g (5 oz) **pancetta**, cubed
1 **onion**, finely chopped
200 g (7 oz) pack **vacuum-packed cooked chestnuts**
150 g (5 oz) **arborio, carnaroli** or **vialone nano rice**
500 ml (17 fl oz) **chicken stock**
150 ml (¼ pint) **milk**
salt and **pepper**

Melt half the butter in a saucepan over a medium heat. Add the pancetta and onion and cook for 10 minutes. Cut the chestnuts in half and add to the pan with the rice and stock. Bring to the boil, then reduce the heat and simmer for 20 minutes, or until most of the liquid has been absorbed and the rice is tender.

Heat the milk in a small saucepan until tepid, then stir into the rice with the remaining butter and season the dish with salt and pepper. Cover and leave to stand for 5 minutes before serving.

For fennel, rice & pancetta soup with garlic & anchovies, follow the recipe above, but replace the onion with 1 large fennel bulb, thinly sliced, omit the chestnuts and replace the milk with 5 tablespoons of the Garlic Anchovy Dip on page 50.

pumpkin & garlic soup

Serves **6–8**
Preparation time **30 minutes**
Cooking time **45 minutes**

750 g (1½ lb) **pumpkin**, peeled, deseeded and cubed
6 **garlic cloves**, unpeeled
4 tablespoons **olive oil**
2 **onions**, thinly sliced
2 **celery sticks**, chopped
50 g (2 oz) **long-grain rice**
1.5 litres (2½ pints) **chicken** or **vegetable stock**, plus extra if needed
4 tablespoons chopped **flat leaf parsley**
salt and **pepper**

Put the pumpkin in a large roasting tin with the garlic cloves and toss with 2 tablespoons of the oil. Roast in a preheated oven, 200°C (400°F), Gas Mark 6, for about 30 minutes until the pumpkin is very tender and beginning to brown.

Meanwhile, heat the remaining oil in a large saucepan over a low heat. Add the onions and celery and cook for 10 minutes until just beginning to brown. Stir in the rice and stock. Bring to the boil, then reduce the heat, cover and simmer for 15–20 minutes until the rice is tender.

Leave the pumpkin and garlic to cool slightly, then pop the garlic cloves out of their skins and mash them with a fork. Add to the saucepan with the pumpkin and bring to the boil, then simmer for 10 minutes.

Roughly blend the soup in a food processor or blender and return to the pan. Season with salt and pepper. Add extra stock if too thick. Reheat and stir in the parsley. Serve with Parmesan Crisps (see below), if liked.

For Parmesan crisps, to serve as an accompaniment, spoon 125 g (4 oz) Parmesan cheese in small mounds on to a baking sheet lined with nonstick baking parchment. Flatten with the back of a spoon. Sprinkle some fennel seeds and finely chopped chilli on top, if liked. Bake in the same oven as the pumpkin and garlic for 3–6 minutes until golden. Remove and leave for 2 minutes to set, or curl over a rolling pin. Carefully lift off the paper or rolling pin and leave to cool completely. Serve separately or sprinkled over the soup.

seafood & fregola soup

Serves **4**
Preparation time **20 minutes**
Cooking time **20 minutes**

- 1.5 litres (2½ pints) **fish stock**
- 250 g (8 oz) **dried fregola** or other **dried small pasta shape**
- 4 tablespoons **extra virgin olive oil**
- 150 g (5 oz) **cherry tomatoes**, halved
- 2 **garlic cloves**, sliced
- 3 **anchovy fillets in olive oil**, drained and roughly chopped
- ¼ teaspoon **crushed dried chillies**
- 100 ml (3½ fl oz) **dry white wine**
- 500 g (1 lb) **mussels**, cleaned (see page 14)
- 375 g (12 oz) **clams**, cleaned (see page 14)
- 300 g (10 oz) **squid rings**
- 12 **raw shelled king prawns**
- 4 tablespoons roughly chopped **flat leaf parsley**
- **salt** (optional)

Bring the stock to the boil in a saucepan, add the pasta and cook for 14–16 minutes, or according to the packet instructions, until al dente.

Meanwhile, heat the oil in a large frying pan or wok over a low heat. Add the tomatoes, garlic, anchovies and crushed chillies and cook for 5 minutes, or until the anchovies have melted into the pan and you can smell the aroma of the garlic.

Pour in the wine, bring to the boil and boil for 1 minute. Add all the seafood and cook, stirring, for 4–5 minutes until the mussels and clams have opened. Discard any that remain closed.

Tip the seafood mixture into the pan with the pasta. Add the parsley, season with salt, if necessary, and stir well. Serve immediately.

For pancetta, potato & fregola soup, cook the pasta as above, but replace the fish stock with 1.5 litres (2½ pints) chicken or vegetable stock. Heat 1 tablespoon olive oil in a separate saucepan. Add 1 chopped onion, 2 sliced celery sticks and 100 g (3½ oz) cubed pancetta and cook over a low heat for 5 minutes. Add 300 g (10 oz) peeled, cubed potatoes and 100 ml (3½ fl oz) dry white wine. Cook for about 10 minutes until the potatoes are tender, then add this mixture to the pan with the pasta. Serve with a drizzle of extra virgin olive oil.

white bean soup

Serves 6
Preparation time **35 minutes**
Cooking time **1 hour 10 minutes**

250 g (8 oz) **dried white beans**, such as haricot or cannellini, soaked overnight in cold water
chicken or **vegetable stock** (optional)
handful of **sage leaves**
75 ml (3 fl oz) **olive oil**
2 **garlic cloves**, finely chopped
2 tablespoons chopped **sage** or **rosemary**
salt and **pepper**

To garnish
roughly chopped **flat leaf parsley**
Toasted Garlic & Chilli Oil (optional)

Drain the beans and put in a flameproof casserole with a tight-fitting lid. Cover with stock or water to a depth of 5 cm (2 inches) above the beans and push in the sage leaves. Bring to the boil, then cover and bake in a preheated oven, 160°C (325°F), Gas Mark 3, for about 1 hour, or until tender. The beans may not take this long, depending on their freshness, so test after 40 minutes. Leave in their cooking liquid.

Put half the beans, the cooked sage leaves and all the cooking liquid into a food processor or blender and process until smooth. Pour the purée back into the casserole with the remaining beans. Add extra stock or water if too thick.

Heat the oil in a frying pan over a low heat. Add the garlic and cook, stirring, until soft and golden. Add the chopped sage or rosemary and cook, stirring, for 30 seconds. Stir into the soup and reheat until boiling, then simmer gently for 10 minutes. Season well with salt and pepper. Serve immediately, garnished with chopped parsley and drizzled with Toasted Garlic & Chilli Oil (see below), if liked.

For toasted garlic & chilli oil, to serve as an accompaniment, heat 75 ml (3 fl oz) olive oil in a frying pan. Add 4 thinly sliced garlic cloves and cook over a medium heat until golden (don't let it overbrown or it will become bitter), then stir in a large pinch of dried chilli flakes. Spoon the garlic and oil over the soup.

tomato & bread soup

Serves **4**
Preparation time **15 minutes**
Cooking time **40 minutes**

2 tablespoons **olive oil**
1 small **onion**, finely chopped
1 **celery stick**, thinly sliced
250 g (8 oz) **day-old rustic bread**, sliced and crusts removed
3 **garlic cloves**, crushed
1 kg (2 lb) **ripe tomatoes**, roughly chopped
1 litre (1¾ pints) **vegetable or chicken stock**
12 **cherry tomatoes**, halved
15 large **basil leaves**
extra virgin olive oil, for drizzling
salt

Heat the oil in a large, heavy-based saucepan over a low heat. Add the onion and celery and cook for 10 minutes until softened and translucent.

Meanwhile, lightly toast the bread until dried and just beginning to colour, then break it into chunks.

Add the garlic to the saucepan and cook, stirring, for 1 minute, then tip in the toasted bread and tomatoes and cook for 5 minutes until the bread disintegrates into the tomatoes. Stir in the stock and simmer gently for 15 minutes. Add the cherry tomatoes and half the basil and simmer for a further 5 minutes.

Season with salt, cover and leave to stand for 5 minutes. Drizzle with extra virgin olive oil and scatter with the remaining basil to serve.

For roasted tomato, bread & balsamic soup, put all the ingredients listed above, except for the bread, stock and extra virgin olive oil, in a roasting tin with 1 tablespoon balsamic vinegar. Drizzle with olive oil and season with salt and pepper. Roast in a preheated oven, 160°C (325°F), Gas Mark 3, for 45 minutes until thickened and caramelized. Bring the stock to the boil in a saucepan, stir in the roasted vegetables and return to the boil. Divide the toasted bread chunks between 4 soup bowls and spoon over the soup. Serve with an extra drizzle of balsamic vinegar.

fennel soup with olive gremolata

Serves **4**
Preparation time **20 minutes**
Cooking time **40 minutes**

75 ml (3 fl oz) **extra virgin olive oil**
3 **spring onions**, chopped
250 g (8 oz) **fennel**, trimmed, cored and thinly sliced, reserving any green fronds for the gremolata and chopping them finely
1 **potato**, diced
finely grated rind and juice of 1 **lemon**
750 ml (1¼ pints) **chicken** or **vegetable stock**
salt and **pepper**

Gremolata
1 small **garlic clove**, finely chopped
finely grated rind of 1 **lemon**
4 tablespoons chopped **parsley**
16 **black olives**, pitted and chopped

Heat the oil in a large saucepan, add the onions and cook for 5–10 minutes until beginning to soften. Add the fennel, potato and lemon rind, and cook for 5 minutes until the fennel begins to soften. Pour in the stock and bring to the boil. Turn down the heat, cover the pan and simmer for about 25 minutes or until the ingredients are tender.

Make the gremolata: mix together the garlic, lemon rind, chopped fennel fronds and parsley then stir the chopped olives into the herb mixture. Cover and chill.

Liquidize the soup and pass it through a sieve to remove any strings of fennel. The soup should not be too thick, so add more stock if necessary. Return it to the rinsed pan. Taste and season well with salt, pepper and plenty of lemon juice. Pour into warmed bowls and sprinkle each serving with a portion of the gremolata.

For a fennel & almond soup with orange & olive gremolata, add 75 g (3 oz) blanched almonds to the pan with the onions. Complete the recipe as above, omitting the potato. Make the gremolata as above, replacing the lemon with the finely grated rind of 1 orange.

ribollita

Serves **4**
Preparation time **15 minutes**
Cooking time **45 minutes**

625 g (1¼ lb) **cavolo nero** (black cabbage)
2 tablespoons **extra virgin olive oil**, plus extra for drizzling
2 **celery sticks**, diced
1 **onion**, thinly sliced
1 large **carrot**, finely chopped
400 g (13 oz) **potatoes**, finely diced
400 g (13 oz) can **plum tomatoes**, drained
400 g (13 oz) can **cannellini beans**, drained and rinsed
1 **bay leaf**
4 **thyme sprigs**
1.5 litres (2½ pints) **vegetable** or **chicken stock**
4 slices of **stale ciabatta bread**, torn into bite-sized pieces
salt and **pepper**

Remove the thick stalks of the cabbage by holding the stems with one hand and using the other hand to strip away the leaves. Discard the stalks and roughly shred the leaves.

Heat the oil in a saucepan over a low heat. Add the celery, onion and carrot and cook for 8–10 minutes until soft and translucent. Stir in the cabbage, potatoes, tomatoes, half the cannellini beans, the bay leaf and thyme, then pour in the stock, season with salt and pepper and bring to the boil. Reduce the heat and simmer, covered, for 30 minutes, until the vegetables are meltingly tender and the stock richly flavoured.

Use a potato masher or fork to mash the remaining beans, then add to the soup, stirring well. Add the bread and continue stirring while it soaks up the soup. The ribollita should be thick enough so that it can be eaten with a fork, but if it starts to look dry, add a little water. Serve with a generous drizzle of oil.

For spring ribollita, follow the recipe above, but omit the cabbage. Cut 1 courgette into cubes and 100 g (3½ oz) French beans into 3.5 cm (1½ inch) pieces, then stir into the pan after the stock has come to the boil, together with 100 g (3½ oz) shelled broad beans. Complete the recipe as above.

clam & courgette soup

Serves **4**
Preparation time **15 minutes**
Cooking time **1 hour 20 minutes**

750 g (1½ lb) fresh **baby clams** or **cockles**, cleaned (see page 14)
3 tablespoons **olive oil**
2 large **garlic cloves**, 1 finely chopped and 1 bruised
750 g (1½ lb) **courgettes**, thickly sliced
finely grated rind and juice of 1 **lemon**
1 tablespoon chopped **marjoram**
1 litre (1¾ pints) **vegetable stock** or **water**
4 thick slices **bread**, toasted
salt and **pepper**
extra olive oil, to serve

Bring 1 cm (½ inch) water to the boil in a saucepan, add the clams and steam until they open. Reserve the juice and remove half of the clams from their shells, keeping the remaining clams in their shells. Discard any clams that have not opened.

Heat the olive oil in a saucepan, add the chopped garlic and cook gently until golden but not brown. Add the courgettes, lemon rind and marjoram and turn them in the oil and garlic. Pour in the stock, season lightly with salt and pepper and bring to simmering point. Cover the pan and simmer for about 10 minutes or until the courgettes are soft.

Pass the soup through a coarse food mill and return it to the pan. Add the reserved clam juice and the shelled clams. If the soup is too thick, add extra stock or water. Taste and season with salt and pepper and a little lemon juice. Stir in the clams in their shells.

Rub the toasted bread with the bruised garlic clove. Place a slice in each bowl and ladle on the soup. Drizzle each serving with olive oil and serve immediately.

For spiced king prawn & courgette soup, replace the clams with 500 g (1 lb) shelled raw king prawns. Follow step 2 and pass the soup through a food mill. Heat 2 tablespoons olive oil in a large frying pan and use to fry the prawns with 2 crushed garlic cloves and a large pinch of crushed dried chillies for 3 minutes, until golden. Add 125 ml (4 oz) dry white wine, boil for 1 minute then season with salt and stir into the soup. Serve with toast and a drizzle of olive oil, as above.

radicchio risotto with pancetta

Serves **4**
Preparation time **10 minutes**
Cooking time **40 minutes**

4 slices of **pancetta**
50 g (2 oz) **salted butter**
1 **onion**, finely chopped
2 **garlic cloves**, finely chopped
200 g (7 oz) **arborio, carnaroli** or **vialone nano rice**
400 ml (14 fl oz) **Barolo** or other full-bodied red wine
175 g (6 oz) **radicchio**, sliced
600 ml (1 pint) **vegetable** or **chicken stock**, simmering
3 tablespoons freshly grated **Parmesan cheese**, plus extra to serve

Cook the pancetta on a baking sheet in a preheated oven, 200°C (400°F), Gas Mark 6, for 5–6 minutes, or until golden brown. Set aside.

Melt half the butter in a heavy-based saucepan over a low heat. Add the onion and cook for 10 minutes until softened. Add the garlic and rice and cook, stirring, for 1 minute. Pour in half the wine and cook, stirring, until absorbed. Add the remaining wine and cook, stirring, until absorbed.

Stir in the radicchio and 3 ladlefuls of the simmering stock. Slowly simmer, stirring constantly, until the stock has been absorbed and the rice parts when a wooden spoon is run through it. Add another ladleful of stock and continue to cook, stirring and adding the stock in ladlefuls, for 18–20 minutes until the rice is creamy and almost tender to the bite.

Remove from the heat and add the remaining butter and the Parmesan. Stir vigorously for 15 seconds. Cover with a tight-fitting lid and leave to stand for 1 minute. Serve immediately topped with the pancetta, with extra Parmesan on the side.

For watercress & lemon risotto, follow the recipe above from the second step, replacing the red wine with 200 ml (7 fl oz) dry white wine, omitting the radicchio and using 900 ml (1½ pints) simmering vegetable stock. Once the risotto is cooked, stir in 125 g (4 oz) roughly chopped watercress and the finely grated rind of 1 lemon with the butter and Parmesan. Leave to stand, as above, before serving.

tomatoes stuffed with rice

Serves **4**
Preparation time **15 minutes**, plus standing
Cooking time **35 minutes**

4 large or 8 small **tomatoes**, about 625 g (1¼ lb) in total
2 **garlic cloves**, crushed
75 g (3 oz) **arborio**, **carnaroli** or **vialone nano rice**
6 **basil leaves**, torn
2 tablespoons **extra virgin olive oil**, plus extra for oiling and drizzling
salt and **pepper**

Cut a slice off the stalk end of each tomato and set aside to use as lids. Scoop the pulp out of the tomatoes and chop. Transfer to a large bowl, taking care not to lose any of the tomato juices, and add the garlic, rice and basil. Season with salt and pepper and stir in 1 tablespoon of the oil. Cover and leave to stand at room temperature for 1 hour, for the rice to soak up all the juices.

Stuff the tomatoes with the rice mixture, then transfer to an oiled baking dish. Top with their reserved lids and drizzle with the remaining oil. Bake in a preheated oven, 180°C (350°F), Gas Mark 4, for 35 minutes until the tomatoes are soft and the rice is cooked through. Serve warm or at room temperature.

For tomatoes stuffed with rice, capers, anchovies & olives, prepare the tomatoes as above. For the filling, add 1 tablespoon each chopped flat leaf parsley, pitted black olives and rinsed capers in brine to the chopped tomato pulp with the garlic and rice. Toss in 2 drained, chopped anchovy fillets in olive oil and season with pepper only. Complete the recipe as above.

pumpkin, sage & chilli risotto

Serves **6**
Preparation time **20 minutes**
Cooking time **40 minutes**

100 g (3½ oz) **butter**
1 large **onion**, finely chopped
1 **fresh** or **dried red chilli**, deseeded and finely chopped
500 g (1 lb) **pumpkin**, peeled, deseeded and roughly chopped
500 g (1 lb) **arborio**, **carnaroli** or **vialone nano rice**
1.5 litres (2½ pints) **chicken** or **vegetable stock**, simmering
3 tablespoons chopped **sage**, plus extra sprigs to garnish
75 g (3 oz) **Parmesan cheese**, freshly grated
salt and **pepper**

Melt half the butter in a large saucepan over a low heat. Add the onion and cook for 10 minutes until softened. Add the chilli and cook, stirring, for 1 minute. Add the pumpkin and cook, stirring constantly, for 5 minutes.

Add the rice and cook, stirring, for 2 minutes. Add a large ladleful of the simmering stock. Slowly simmer, stirring constantly, until the stock has been absorbed and the rice parts when a wooden spoon is run through it. Add another ladleful of stock and continue to cook, stirring and adding the stock in ladlefuls, for about 20 minutes until the rice is creamy and almost tender to the bite and the pumpkin is beginning to disintegrate. Season well with salt and pepper.

Remove from the heat and add the chopped sage, remaining butter and the Parmesan. Stir vigorously for 15 seconds. Cover with a tight-fitting lid and leave to stand for a few minutes. Serve garnished with sage sprigs.

For pumpkin risotto with amaretto biscuits & almonds, cook the risotto as above, omitting the sage and replacing the Parmesan with 2 crushed amaretto biscuits. Serve with a scattering of toasted almond flakes.

asparagus, pea & mint risotto

Serves **4**
Preparation time **10 minutes**
Cooking time **45 minutes**

500 g (1 lb) **asparagus spears**
1 litre (1¾ pints) **vegetable or fish stock**
50 g (2 oz) **butter**
1 **onion**, finely chopped
300 g (10 oz) **arborio, carnaroli** or **vialone nano rice**
150 ml (¼ pint) **dry white wine**
100 g (3½ oz) shelled **fresh or frozen peas**
4 tablespoons freshly grated **Parmesan cheese**, plus extra to serve
handful of **mint leaves**, roughly chopped

Cut the asparagus in half, at an angle, separating the tips from the thicker stalks. Reserve the tips. Put the stalks in a saucepan with the stock and bring to the boil. Boil for 5 minutes, then reduce the heat to a simmer. Remove the asparagus with a slotted spoon and process in a food processor or blender until puréed.

Melt half the butter in a heavy-based saucepan over a low heat. Add the onion and cook for 10 minutes until softened. Add the rice and cook, stirring, for 1 minute. Add the wine and cook, stirring, until absorbed. Stir in the puréed asparagus.

Add 2 ladlefuls of the simmering stock. Slowly simmer, stirring constantly, until the stock has been absorbed and the rice parts when a wooden spoon is run through it. Add another ladleful of stock and continue to cook, stirring and adding the stock in ladlefuls, reserving 2 ladlefuls, for 16–18 minutes until the rice is creamy and almost tender to the bite.

Add the peas and the reserved asparagus tips and stock and continue cooking until the stock is almost absorbed. Remove from the heat and stir in the Parmesan, mint and remaining butter. Stir vigorously for 15 seconds. Cover with a tight-fitting lid and leave to stand for 2 minutes. Serve immediately with extra Parmesan on the side.

For asparagus & pancetta risotto, follow the recipe above, but cook 150 g (5 oz) cubed pancetta with the onion. Omit the peas and replace the mint with 2 tablespoons roughly chopped flat leaf parsley.

saffron risotto

Serves **4**
Preparation time **5 minutes**
Cooking time **35 minutes**

50 g (2 oz) **butter**
1 **onion**, finely chopped
300 g (10 oz) **arborio, carnaroli** or **vialone nano rice**
150 ml (¼ pint) **dry white wine**
1 litre (1¾ pints) **beef** or **vegetable stock**, simmering
½ teaspoon **saffron threads**
4 tablespoons freshly grated **Parmesan cheese**, plus extra to serve

Melt half the butter in a heavy-based saucepan over a low heat. Add the onion and cook for 10 minutes until softened. Add the rice and cook, stirring, for 1 minute. Pour in the wine and cook, stirring, until absorbed.

Add 2 ladlefuls of the simmering stock and the saffron. Slowly simmer, stirring constantly, until the stock has been absorbed and the rice parts when a wooden spoon is run through it. Add another ladleful of stock and continue to cook, stirring and adding the stock in ladlefuls, for 18–20 minutes until the rice is creamy and almost tender to the bite.

Remove from the heat and stir in the Parmesan and remaining butter. Stir vigorously for 15 seconds. Cover with a tight-fitting lid and leave to stand for 1 minute. Serve immediately with extra Parmesan on the side.

For prawn, courgette & saffron risotto, follow the recipe above, but when the rice has been cooking for 15 minutes and most of the stock has been incorporated, stir 1 roughly grated courgette and 16 raw shelled king prawns into the rice mixture. Continue adding the remaining stock and complete the recipe as above, but omit the Parmesan.

baked polenta with gorgonzola

Serves **4**
Preparation time **5 minutes**
Cooking time **15 minutes**

750 ml (1¼ pints) **water**
225 g (7½ oz) **instant polenta**
50 g (2 oz) **butter**, plus extra for greasing
200 g (7 oz) **Gorgonzola cheese**, broken into pieces
5 tablespoons freshly grated **Parmesan cheese**
10 **cherry tomatoes**
salt and **pepper**

Bring the measurement water to the boil in a large, heavy-based saucepan. Set aside 2 tablespoons of the polenta to use for the topping and put the remaining polenta in a jug. Pour into the water in a slow but steady stream, stirring vigorously with a wooden spoon to prevent any lumps forming. Reduce the heat to a slow simmer and cook, stirring frequently, for about 5 minutes, or until the polenta is thick and comes away from the side of the pan. Stir in the butter and season with salt and pepper.

Pour half the polenta into a greased baking dish, about 25 x 18 cm (10 x 7 inches). Top with the Gorgonzola and half the Parmesan. Cover with the remaining cooked polenta, then top with the tomatoes. Stir the remaining Parmesan into the reserved uncooked polenta for the topping and scatter over the dish.

Cook under a preheated medium grill for 4–5 minutes until the tomatoes are slightly softened and beginning to char. Serve steaming hot.

For griddled herbed polenta, cook the polenta as in the first step, then stir in 2 tablespoons each roughly chopped flat leaf parsley, basil and wild rocket leaves and add 4 tablespoons grated Parmesan cheese. Tip into a 1 kg (2 lb) loaf tin and leave to cool at room temperature. Turn the polenta out and cut into 1 cm (½ inch) slices. Brush with olive oil, then cook on a preheated ridged griddle pan over a high heat for 1 minute on each side.

polenta chips

Serves **4**
Preparation time **15 minutes**, plus chilling
Cooking time **35 minutes**

50 g (2 oz) **butter**
600 ml (1 pint) **water**
1 teaspoon **salt**
125 g (4 oz) **instant polenta**
sunflower oil, for oiling and deep-frying
plain flour, for coating
paprika, for sprinkling
salt

Put the butter, measurement water and salt in a heavy-based saucepan and bring to the boil. Put the polenta in a jug and pour into the water mixture in a slow but steady stream, stirring vigorously with a wooden spoon to prevent lumps forming. Reduce the heat to a slow simmer and cook, stirring frequently, for about 5 minutes, or until the polenta is thick and comes away from the side of the pan.

Transfer the polenta to a shallow oiled dish, smooth the top and leave to cool. Cover and chill until firm.

Turn the polenta out on to wet greaseproof paper and cut into thick chips with a wet knife.

Heat enough oil for deep-frying in a deep saucepan to 180–190°C (350–375°F), or until a cube of bread browns in 30 seconds. Roll the chips in a little flour to coat, add to the hot oil, in batches, and cook for 6–8 minutes until pale golden brown and crisp. Remove with a slotted spoon and drain on kitchen paper. Sprinkle with salt and paprika. Keep warm in a low oven with the door ajar until ready to serve.

For tomato & basil dip, to serve as an accompaniment, blend 4 ripe tomatoes with 1 garlic clove, 4 basil leaves and ½ deseeded red chilli. Stir in 2 tablespoons extra virgin olive oil and season with salt. Serve with the chips, omitting the paprika.

cheesy polenta & mushrooms

Serves **4**
Preparation time **10 minutes**
Cooking time **15 minutes**

400 g (13 oz) **mixed wild mushrooms**, such as porcini, girolles and chanterelles
25 g (1 oz) **butter**
2 **garlic cloves**, chopped
5 whole **sage leaves**
50 ml (2 fl oz) **dry vermouth**
salt and **pepper**

Polenta
750 ml (1 ¼ pints) **water**
200 g (7 oz) **instant polenta**
50 g (2 oz) **Parmesan cheese**, freshly grated
50 g (2 oz) **butter**, cubed

Brush away any soil and grit from the mushrooms with a moist cloth, then slice the porcini and tear any other large mushrooms in half. Set aside.

Melt the butter in a large frying pan over a medium-high heat. Add the garlic, sage and the dense, tougher mushrooms and cook for 2–3 minutes. Add the remaining mushrooms, season with salt and pepper and cook for 2–3 minutes until soft and cooked through. Pour in the vermouth and cook, stirring, for 1 minute.

For the polenta, bring the measurement water to the boil in a large, heavy-based saucepan. Put the polenta in a jug and pour into the water in a slow but steady stream, stirring vigorously with a wooden spoon to prevent any lumps forming. Reduce the heat to a slow simmer and cook, stirring frequently, for about 5 minutes, or until the polenta is thick and comes away from the side of the pan. Stir in the butter and season with salt and pepper.

Divide the polenta between 4 serving plates, then top with the mushrooms.

For cheesy polenta with mushrooms & tomato, cook the mushrooms as above, but replace the rosemary with 3 chopped thyme sprigs and use 150 ml (¼ pint) full-bodied red wine instead of the vermouth. When the wine has boiled for 1 minute, stir in 300 ml (½ pint) passata. Season with salt and pepper and bring to the boil, then simmer for 5 minutes. Cook the polenta as above, then gradually stir in the cheese. Serve with the mushroom and tomato mixture.

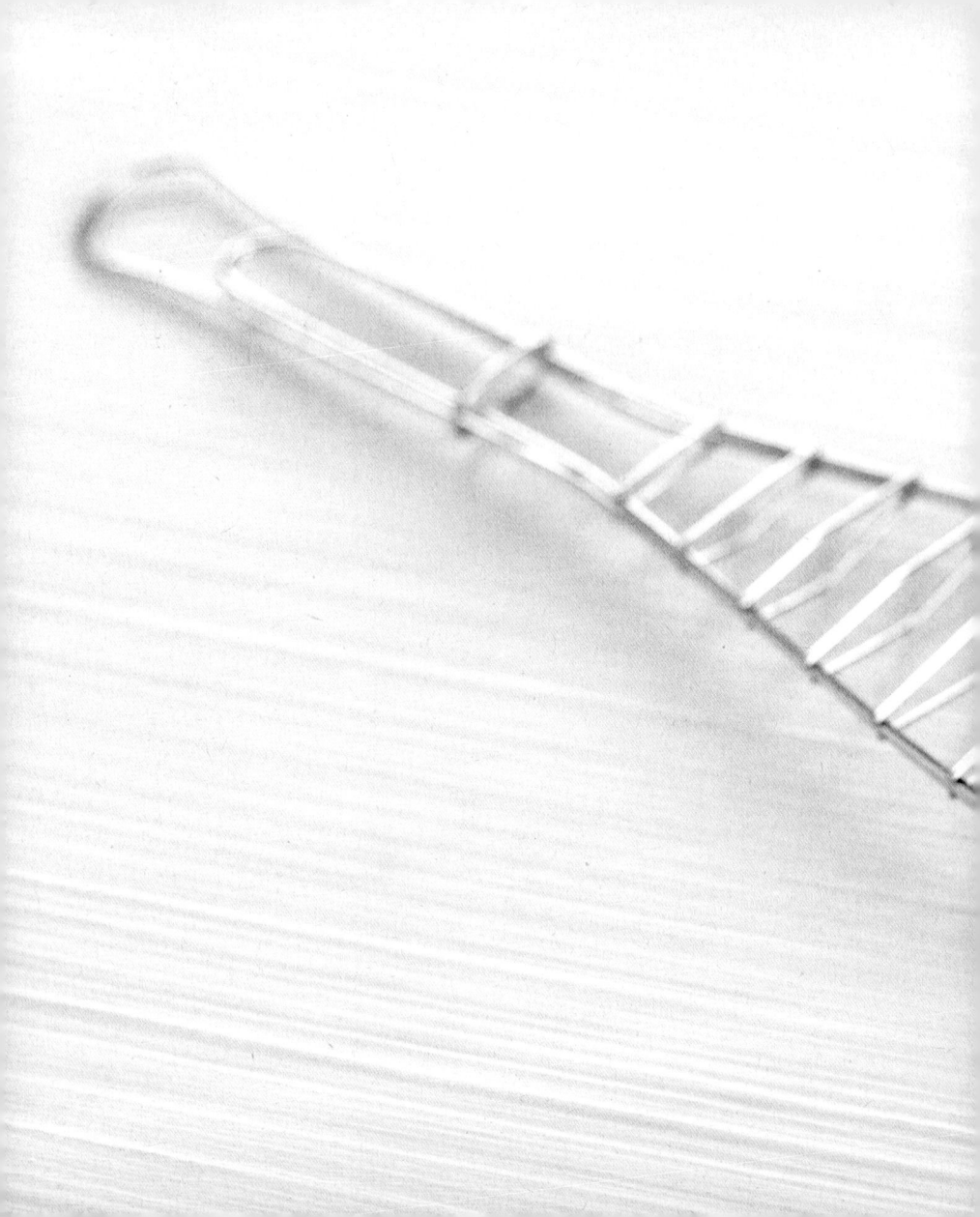

fish & seafood

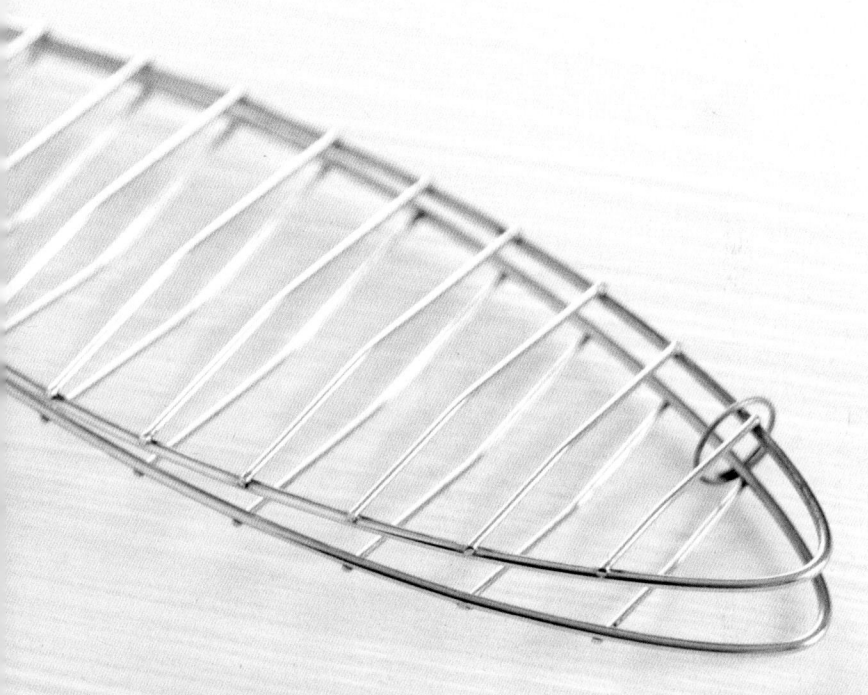

sea bass in a salt crust

Serves **4**
Preparation time **15 minutes**
Cooking time **30 minutes**

1 **sea bass**, about 450 g (14½ oz), gutted and scaled
1 kg (2 lb) **coarse sea salt**
1 **egg white**
1 tablespoon **cold water**

To serve
lemon wedges
extra virgin olive oil

Wash the inside and outside of the sea bass under cold running water and pat dry with kitchen paper.

Put the sea salt in a bowl. Whisk the egg white and measurement water together in a small bowl, then stir into the sea salt.

Spread a layer of the sea salt mixture out in the base of a roasting tin large enough to hold the fish comfortably. Lay the fish on top, then cover the fish with the remaining salt mixture. Pat down, making sure that the fish is completely encased by the salt.

Roast in a preheated oven, 200°C (400°F), Gas Mark 6, for 30 minutes. Remove from the oven. Break the salt crust with the back of a large knife and lift off. If there are still a lot of salt crystals on the surface of the fish, brush these off with a pastry brush. Use a fish slice to lift the fish on to a serving dish. Serve with lemon wedges and extra virgin olive oil for drizzling, accompanied by steamed vegetables.

For fennel, lemon & thyme sea bass in a salt crust, pound 2 teaspoons fennel seeds, the finely grated rind of 1 lemon, the leaves of 3 thyme sprigs and 1 tablespoon olive oil in a mortar with a pestle. Rub the mixture all over the inside and outside of the sea bass. Cover and leave to marinate in the refrigerator for 30 minutes. Prepare the salt mixture and roast the fish in the salt crust as above.

red mullet with salsa verde

Serves **4**
Preparation time **20 minutes**
Cooking time **10 minutes**

4 **red mullet**, gutted and scaled
2 tablespoons **olive oil**
1 **lemon**, halved lengthways and thinly sliced
salt and **pepper**

Salsa verde
2 **garlic cloves**, finely chopped
3 **anchovy fillets in olive oil**, finely chopped
1 tablespoon **capers in brine**, rinsed and finely chopped
4 tablespoons roughly chopped **flat leaf parsley**
2 tablespoons roughly chopped **mint**
2 tablespoons roughly chopped **basil**
1 tablespoon **red wine vinegar**
4 tablespoons **extra virgin olive oil**

Combine all the ingredients for the salsa verde in a bowl and season with salt and pepper. Set aside.

Wash the inside and outside of the mullet under cold running water and pat dry with kitchen paper. Cut 2–3 deep slashes along the width of both sides of the mullet, then brush the fish all over with the oil. Season with salt and pepper. Insert a lemon slice into each slash, then tuck a couple of slices inside each fish.

Lay the mullet on a nonstick baking sheet and cook under a preheated very high grill, about 10 cm (4 inches) from the heat source, for about 5 minutes on each side until cooked through and lightly charred. Serve immediately with the salsa verde.

For smoked mackerel with potato & salsa verde salad, boil or steam 500 g (1 lb) baby new potatoes until tender, then lightly crush with the back of a spoon. Prepare the salsa verde as above, but using 5 tablespoons extra virgin olive oil. Toss the warm potatoes with the dressing. Replace the red mullet with 4 smoked mackerel fillets. Break into large flakes and gently toss into the salad.

roast garlic-studded monkfish

Serves **4**
Preparation time **20 minutes**, plus marinating
Cooking time **30 minutes**

- 1 kg (2 lb) **monkfish tail**, trimmed and boned (see page 138)
- 3–4 **bay leaves**
- 1 teaspoon **fennel seeds**
- 4 **garlic cloves**, cut into thick slivers
- 4 tablespoons **olive oil**
- a few **thyme sprigs**
- 2 **red peppers**, cored, deseeded and roughly chopped
- 1 **aubergine**, cut into bite-sized chunks
- 2 **courgettes**, cut into bite-sized chunks
- 3 **ripe plum tomatoes**, cut into chunks
- 3 tablespoons **lemon juice**
- **salt** and **pepper**

To garnish
- 2 tablespoons **salted capers**, rinsed and chopped
- 3 tablespoons chopped **flat leaf parsley**

Lay the bay leaves over one monkfish fillet and scatter over the fennel seeds. Lay the other fillet on top and tie at 2.5 cm (1 inch) intervals with fine string. With the tip of a sharp knife, make slits all over the monkfish and push in the garlic slivers. Put the oil, thyme and a little pepper into a glass dish, add the monkfish and turn well to coat. Cover and leave to marinate in the refrigerator for at least 2 hours or overnight.

Remove from the marinade. Pour 2 tablespoons of the marinade into a heavy, nonstick frying pan and heat until almost smoking. Add the monkfish and cook, turning, for 2–3 minutes until sealed. Set aside.

Heat the remaining marinade in the pan. Add the vegetables and quickly brown. Transfer to a heavy, shallow baking dish, set the monkfish on top and add the tomatoes and lemon juice. Bake in a preheated oven, 220°C (425°F), Gas Mark 7, for 20 minutes, basting and turning the vegetables occasionally.

Remove the string and cut the fish into thick slices. Season the vegetables with salt and pepper. Serve the monkfish on the vegetables, garnished with the capers and parsley.

For roasted monkfish with olive paste, omit the marinade. Make a quick olive paste by blending 100 g (3½ oz) pitted black olives, the leaves from 2 sprigs thyme, 1 garlic clove and 3 tablespoons olive oil. Spread over one monkfish fillet then lay the other fillet on top and tie as above. Seal the monkfish in a pan with 2 tablespoons olive oil then roast it with the vegetables, as above.

sole with tomatoes & capers

Serves **2**
Preparation time **10 minutes**
Cooking time **25 minutes**

4 tablespoons **olive oil**
1 **garlic clove**, roughly chopped
2 **Dover sole**, about 400 g (13 oz) each, skinned (ask your fishmonger to do this for you)
50 g (2 oz) **plain flour**, seasoned with **salt**
100 ml (3½ fl oz) **dry white wine**
200 ml (7 fl oz) **passata**
pinch of **caster sugar**
½ teaspoon **dried oregano**
2 tablespoons **capers in brine**, rinsed
salt and **pepper** (optional)

Heat the oil in a large frying pan over a low heat. Add the garlic and cook for 10 minutes. Discard the garlic and increase the heat to high.

Pat the sole dry with kitchen paper, then turn in the seasoned flour to coat both sides. Gently lower into the hot oil and cook for 4–5 minutes on each side until golden (if your pan isn't large enough, cook individually and keep the cooked sole warm in a low oven while you cook the remaining fish). Remove to a warmed serving plate.

Pour the wine into the frying pan and cook, stirring well with a wooden spoon to loosen any sediment from the base of the pan, for 1 minute. Add the passata, sugar, oregano and capers and bring to the boil. Check the seasoning and add salt and pepper if necessary, then spoon the sauce over the fish. Serve immediately.

For sole with lemon, parsley & garlic, cook the sole as above and keep warm. Melt 50 g (2 oz) butter in the frying pan over a medium heat and stir in the grated rind of 1 lemon and 2 crushed garlic cloves. Cook for 2 minutes, then remove from the heat and stir in the juice of 1 lemon and 2 tablespoons finely chopped flat leaf parsley. Spoon over the fish and serve immediately.

sardines stuffed with fennel

Serves **4**
Preparation time **15 minutes**, plus cooling
Cooking time **25 minutes**

4 tablespoons **extra virgin olive oil**
1 **fennel bulb**, thinly sliced
1 **onion**, thinly sliced
pared **rind** of 1 small **orange**
pared **rind** of 1 **lemon**
1 tablespoon roughly chopped **dill**
1 teaspoon **fennel seeds**
¼ teaspoon **crushed dried chillies**
2 **garlic cloves**, finely chopped
5 tablespoons **fresh white breadcrumbs**
2 tablespoons roughly chopped **flat leaf parsley**
4 large or 8 small **sardines**, filleted
juice of ½ **lemon**
salt
lemon wedges, to serve

Pour half the oil into a large, heavy-based frying pan and stir in the fennel and onion. Add the citrus rind, dill, fennel seeds and crushed chillies and place the pan over a very low heat. Cook, stirring frequently, for 12–15 minutes until the fennel and onion are golden and caramelized, being careful not to burn. Add the garlic and cook, stirring, for 2 minutes. Remove from the heat and stir in half the breadcrumbs and parsley. Season with salt and leave to cool.

Drizzle 1 tablespoon of the remaining oil over a large baking sheet. Add half the sardine fillets, skin-side down. Season lightly with salt, then spread the fennel mixture over each fillet. Press a second fillet on top, skin-side up, and scatter with the remaining breadcrumbs and parsley. Drizzle with the remaining oil and squeeze the lemon juice over the fish. Season again with salt.

Cook under a preheated high grill for 6–8 minutes until the fish is opaque all the way through. Serve with lemon wedges, accompanied by a tomato and lettuce salad.

For spaghetti with sardine & fennel sauce, cook 400 g (13 oz) dried spaghetti in a large saucepan of salted boiling water for 8–10 minutes, or according to the packet instructions, until al dente. Meanwhile, follow the first step above, omitting the breadcrumbs and adding 250 g (8 oz) roughly chopped sardine fillets to the pan with the garlic. Cook for 2 minutes until cooked through. Drain the pasta, return to the pan and stir through the sauce.

monkfish in salsa d'agrumi

Serves **4**
Preparation time **20 minutes**
Cooking time **15 minutes**

875 g (1¾ lb) **monkfish tail**
plain flour, seasoned with **salt** and **pepper**, for coating
2 tablespoons **olive oil**
finely grated **rind** and **juice** of 1 **lemon**
finely grated **rind** and **juice** of 1 **orange**
150 ml (¼ pint) **dry white wine**
2 tablespoons chopped **flat leaf parsley**
salt and **pepper**

To garnish
pared **orange rind**
parsley sprigs
orange and **lemon wedges**

Trim any membrane and dark meat from the monkfish. Remove the central bone by slitting the fish down the centre until you reach the bone. Turn the fish over and do the same on the other side. Ease out the bone, gently scraping the flesh away with the tip of a knife. Cut the fish into large chunks, then toss in seasoned flour to coat all over, shaking off the excess.

Heat the oil in a nonstick frying pan over a medium-high heat. Add the fish and cook until golden all over. Remove to a plate.

Add the grated citrus rind and juice to the pan with the wine and boil rapidly. Reduce the heat, return the fish to the pan and simmer gently for 3–4 minutes, or until the fish is cooked through. Stir in the parsley and salt and pepper to taste.

Lift the fish out on to a warmed serving dish. Boil the sauce to reduce it a little more, then pour over the fish. Serve immediately, garnished with orange rind, parsley sprigs and orange and lemon wedges.

For sole in lemon & basil sauce, dust 2 x 400 g (13 oz) skinned Dover sole in seasoned plain flour and fry in the oil, instead of the monkfish, for 2 minutes on each side, until golden. Remove to a plate then continue the recipe as above, omitting the orange juice and rind and adding 5 torn basil leaves to the sauce instead of the parsley.

swordfish with onion & sultanas

Serves **4**
Preparation time **10 minutes**
Cooking time **20 minutes**

4 tablespoons **olive oil**
1 **onion**, thinly sliced
1 **celery stick**, sliced
2 tablespoons **sultanas**
1 **bay leaf**
3 tablespoons **pine nuts**
2 **garlic cloves**, sliced
4 **swordfish steaks**, about 2.5 cm (1 inch) thick
plain flour, seasoned with **salt** and **pepper**, for coating
150 ml (¼ pint) **dry white wine**

Heat half the oil in a large, heavy-based frying pan over a low heat. Add the onion, celery, sultanas and bay leaf and cook for 8–10 minutes until soft and golden. Stir in the pine nuts and garlic and cook for a further 2 minutes. Remove to a dish.

Heat the remaining oil in the pan over a high heat. Turn the swordfish steaks in the seasoned flour to coat on both sides. Add to the hot oil and cook for 3 minutes on each side until golden brown.

Return the onion mixture to the pan and pour in the wine. Boil vigorously for 2 minutes. Serve immediately.

For tuna with onion & olives, follow the first step above, but omit the sultanas and replace the pine nuts with 50 g (2 oz) halved, pitted black olives. Continue with the recipe as above, but use 4 tuna steaks, about 2.5 cm (1 inch) thick, instead of the swordfish steaks.

barbecued prawn skewers

Serves **4**
Preparation time **10 minutes**, plus marinating
Cooking time **5 minutes**

1 **garlic clove**, sliced
3 tablespoons **extra virgin olive oil**
1 tablespoon chopped **flat leaf parsley**
finely grated **rind** of 1 **lemon**
20 raw **king prawns**
salt
lemon wedges, to serve

Put the garlic, oil, parsley and lemon rind in a non-reactive bowl and toss in the prawns. Cover and leave to marinate in the refrigerator for at least 15 minutes and up to 1 hour.

Heat a ridged griddle pan over a high heat until smoking hot, or preheat a gas barbecue to high or, if using a charcoal barbecue, get the coals to the stage where there are no more flames and the coals are covered with a thin layer of grey ash.

Thread the prawns on to metal skewers and season with salt. Cook for 1–2 minutes on each side until the prawns have turned pink and are lightly charred. Serve immediately with lemon wedges.

For tomato, onion & bread salad, to serve as an accompaniment, stir ½ thinly sliced red onion, 500 g (1 lb) quartered tomatoes and 5 torn basil leaves into a bowl with 3 tablespoons extra virgin olive oil and 1 tablespoon red wine vinegar. Season with salt and pepper and toss in 75 g (3 oz) stale rustic bread, cut into walnut-sized pieces. Cover and leave to marinate at room temperature for 30 minutes before serving.

mussels alla marinara

Serves **4**
Preparation time **15 minutes**
Cooking time **10 minutes**

3 tablespoons **olive oil**
4 **garlic cloves**, chopped
150 ml (¼ pint) **dry white wine**
400 g (13 oz) can **chopped tomatoes**
1 small **red chilli**, deseeded and finely chopped
2 tablespoons chopped **flat leaf parsley**, plus extra whole leaves to garnish
2 kg (4 lb) **mussels**, cleaned (see page 14)
salt and **pepper**

Heat the oil in a large saucepan over a low heat. Add the garlic and cook for about 5 minutes until golden. Add the wine, tomatoes, chilli and chopped parsley and bring to the boil. Season well with salt and pepper.

Add the mussels to the pan, cover and cook over a high heat, shaking the pan frequently, for 4–5 minutes, or until the shells have opened. Stir well and discard any that remain closed.

Scatter the whole parsley leaves over the mussels and serve immediately with crusty bread, if liked.

For squid alla marinara, fry the garlic as above, also adding ½ teaspoon fennel seeds to the pan. Continue following the recipe, replacing the mussels with 500 g (1 lb) squid rings.

stuffed squid in tomato sauce

Serves **4**
Preparation time **15 minutes**, plus cooling
Cooking time **45 minutes**

8 **squid**, about 625 g (1¼ lb) in total, cleaned (see page 14)
4 tablespoons **olive oil**
400 g (13 oz) can **chopped tomatoes**
100 ml (3½ fl oz) **dry white wine**

Filling
2 teaspoons **olive oil**
1 small **onion**, finely chopped
2 **anchovy fillets in olive oil**, drained and roughly chopped
2 **garlic cloves**, crushed
100 g (3½ oz) **fresh white breadcrumbs**
2 tablespoons roughly chopped **flat leaf parsley**, plus extra to garnish
large pinch of **crushed dried chillies**
salt

Pull the squid wings away from the body cavities. Roughly chop the wings and the tentacles and set aside.

For the filling, heat the oil in a frying pan over a medium heat. Add the onion and anchovies and cook for 8 minutes until the onion is soft and translucent. Stir in the chopped squid and garlic and cook, stirring for 1 minute. Leave to cool, then stir in the remaining filling ingredients.

Stuff the squid body cavities with the filling, using a teaspoon to help push the filling in. Fill only three-quarters of the way up, then secure the ends with cocktail sticks.

Heat the oil in a large, heavy-based frying pan over a high heat. Add the squid and cook for 1–2 minutes on each side until golden brown. Pour in the tomatoes and wine and bring to the boil. Reduce the heat and simmer for 25–30 minutes until the sauce has thickened and the squid is so tender that it offers no resistance when pricked with a fork. Serve garnished with chopped parsley, accompanied by steamed potatoes or soft polenta.

For barbecued stuffed squid, stuff the squid as above, also adding 1 tablespoon chopped mint and the finely grated rind of 1 lemon to the filling. Cook over a gas barbecue preheated to high or over a charcoal barbecue with coals covered with a thin layer of grey ash for 3–4 minutes on each side. Serve with a squeeze of lemon and a drizzle of extra virgin olive oil.

fried calamari

Serves **4**
Preparation time **15 minutes**
Cooking time **10 minutes**

1 kg (2 lb) **squid**, cleaned (see page 14)
vegetable oil, for deep-frying
75 g (3 oz) **plain flour**
salt
lemon wedges, to serve

Cut the squid bodies into rings. Dry the rings and the tentacles thoroughly with kitchen paper.

Heat enough oil for deep-frying in a deep saucepan to 180–190°C (350–375°F), or until a cube of bread browns in 30 seconds. Season the squid with salt, then coat half in the flour, shaking off any excess. Add to the hot oil and cook for 2–3 minutes, or until golden and crisp. Remove with a slotted spoon and drain on kitchen paper. Scatter with a pinch of salt. Repeat with the remaining squid. Serve immediately with lemon wedges.

For spicy fried prawns, replace the squid with 20 raw peeled king prawns. Mix ¼ teaspoon cayenne pepper into 100 g (3½ oz) plain flour and make into a batter by stirring in 175 ml (6 fl oz) ice-cold sparkling water. Season the prawns with salt, then coat in the batter and deep-fry in batches, as above, for 4–5 minutes. Drain on kitchen paper and serve with lemon wedges.

meat & poultry

classic meatloaf

Serves **4**
Preparation time **25 minutes**
Cooking time **55 minutes**

- 2 thick slices of **white bread**, crusts removed and broken into chunks
- 2 tablespoons **milk**
- large pinch of freshly grated **nutmeg**
- 500 g (1 lb) **minced beef**
- 6 slices of **pancetta** or **streaky bacon**, finely chopped
- 1 small **onion**, finely chopped
- 3 **garlic cloves**, finely chopped
- 4 tablespoons freshly grated **Parmesan cheese**
- 1 **egg**, lightly beaten
- 100 g (3½ oz) **fine dry white breadcrumbs**
- 2 tablespoons **olive oil**
- 150 ml (¼ pint) **dry white wine**
- 400 g (13 oz) can **chopped tomatoes**
- finely grated **rind** of 1 **orange**
- 2 tablespoons roughly chopped **flat leaf parsley**
- **salt** and **pepper**

Soak the bread in a bowl with the milk and nutmeg for about 10 minutes until the milk is absorbed. Mash with a fork. Combine the beef, pancetta or bacon, onion and half the garlic in a large bowl. Add the Parmesan, egg and bread. Season with salt and pepper. Mix gently with your hands until well combined. Form into a loaf shape. Spread the breadcrumbs out on a large plate and roll the meatloaf over to coat thoroughly.

Heat the oil in a shallow saucepan with a tight-fitting lid over a medium heat. Add the meatloaf and cook, turning occasionally, until golden all over. Add the wine, boil rapidly until reduced by half, then add the tomatoes. Cover and simmer very gently, turning the meatloaf occasionally and adding a little water if necessary, for 40–45 minutes, or until a knife inserted into the centre comes out hot.

Lift on to a serving dish. Stir the orange rind, parsley and remaining garlic into the pan and simmer for 2 minutes. Season with salt and pepper. Spoon over the meatloaf.

For meatballs in red wine sauce, soak the bread, then combine the remaining ingredients as above, omitting the breadcrumbs, oil, wine and tomatoes. Season and shape into golf-ball sized balls. Heat 2 tablespoons olive oil in a frying pan over a medium heat, add the meatballs and cook for 8–10 minutes until golden. Add 200 ml (7 fl oz) full-bodied red wine, boil for 2 minutes, then stir in the tomatoes. Bring to the boil, then simmer, covered, for 20 minutes.

calves' liver & caramelized onions

Serves **4**
Preparation time **10 minutes**
Cooking time **40–45 minutes**

50 g (2 oz) **butter**
2 tablespoons **olive oil**
2 large **onions**, thinly sliced
625 g (1¼ 1b) **calves' liver**, thinly sliced (ask your butcher to slice as thinly as possible)
2 tablespoons finely chopped **flat leaf parsley**
salt and **pepper**

Melt half the butter with the oil in a large frying pan with a tight-fitting lid. Add the onions and season with salt and pepper, then cover and cook over a very low heat, stirring occasionally, for 35–40 minutes until very soft and golden. Remove to a bowl and increase the heat under the pan to high.

Season the liver with salt and pepper and melt the remaining butter in the pan. Once the butter starts foaming, add the liver and cook for 1–2 minutes until browned. Turn over and return the onions to the pan. Cook for a further minute, then serve immediately with the parsley scattered over.

For chicken liver & caramelized onions, cook the onions as above and remove from the pan. Replace the calves' liver with 400 g (13 oz) chicken livers, coated in seasoned flour. Cook the livers in the remaining butter in the pan as above for 4–5 minutes, turning once. Add 1 tablespoon aged balsamic vinegar, swirl in the pan for a couple of seconds, then return the caramelized onions to the pan. Cook for a further minute, stir in the parsley as above and serve immediately.

roast lamb with wine & juniper

Serves **6**
Preparation time **20 minutes**
Cooking time **1 hour 35 minutes**

2 tablespoons **olive oil**
1 **leg of lamb**, about 1.5 kg (3 lb), trimmed of excess fat
10 **juniper berries**, crushed
3 **garlic cloves**, crushed
50 g (2 oz) **salted anchovies**, boned and rinsed
1 tablespoon chopped **rosemary**
2 tablespoons **balsamic vinegar**
2 **rosemary sprigs**
300 ml (½ pint) **dry white wine**
salt and **pepper**

Heat the oil in a roasting tin in which the lamb will fit snugly. Add the lamb and cook until browned all over. Leave to cool.

Pound 6 of the juniper berries, the garlic, anchovies and chopped rosemary with the end of a rolling pin in a bowl. Stir in the vinegar and mix to a paste. Make small incisions all over the lamb with a small, sharp knife. Spread the paste over the lamb, working it into the incisions. Season with salt and pepper. Put the rosemary sprigs in the roasting tin and put the lamb on top. Pour in the wine and add the remaining juniper berries.

Cover the roasting tin with foil and bring to the boil, then cook in a preheated oven, 160°C (325°F), Gas Mark 3, for 1 hour, turning the lamb every 20 minutes. Raise the temperature to 200°C (400°F), Gas Mark 6, uncover and roast for a further 30 minutes until the lamb is very tender.

For leg of lamb with lemon & rosemary, omit the juniper berries and pound the grated zest of 2 lemons, with the garlic, anchovies and rosemary. Replace the vinegar with the juice of 1 lemon. Spoon the sauce over the lamb, as above.

veal escalopes with parma ham

Serves **4**
Preparation time **10 minutes**
Cooking time **10 minutes**

4 **veal escalopes**, about 150 g (5 oz) each
4 slices of **Parma ham**
4 **sage leaves**
plain flour, for dusting
25 g (1 oz) **butter**
2 tablespoons **olive oil**
150 ml (¼ pint) **dry white wine**
salt and **pepper**

Lay the escalopes between 2 sheets of clingfilm and beat with a rolling pin until wafer thin.

Season with salt and pepper, then lay a slice of Parma ham on each escalope, followed by a sage leaf. Secure the sage and ham in position with a cocktail stick, then lightly dust both sides of the veal with flour. Season again with salt and pepper.

Melt the butter with the oil in a large frying pan over a high heat. Add the escalopes and cook for 2–3 minutes on each side until golden brown. Add the wine to the pan and bubble until thickened and reduced by about half. Serve immediately, accompanied by boiled or steamed potatoes and/or a cooked green vegetable.

For chicken breast with rosemary & pancetta, replace the veal with 4 boneless chicken breasts, about 150 g (5 oz) each, skinned. Top each flattened breast with a scattering of rosemary needles, then wrap each in a slice of pancetta, in place of the Parma ham, omitting the sage. Dust with flour, season with salt and pepper and cook as above.

pork braised in milk

Serves **6**
Preparation time **10 minutes**, plus resting
Cooking time **1¾ hours**

25 g (1 oz) **butter**
3 tablespoons **olive oil**
1 **loin of pork with 6 chops**, about 2.25 kg (4½ lb) in total, chined and skin removed (ask your butcher to do this for you)
1 litre (1¾ pints) **milk**
4 **garlic cloves**, peeled but kept whole
pared **rind** of 2 **lemons**
8 **sage leaves**
salt and **pepper**

Melt the butter with the oil in a large, heavy-based flameproof casserole or a roasting tin large enough to hold the pork. Season the pork with salt and pepper and add to the pan, fat-side down. Cook over a medium-high heat for 10 minutes until golden brown.

Pour away most of the fat and turn the pork over, skin-side up. Pour in the milk and add the garlic, lemon rind and sage. Bring to the boil, then cover with a lid or foil, leaving a little gap for the steam to escape. Cook on the hob over a very low heat or in a preheated oven, 150°C (300°F), Gas Mark 2, for 1½ hours, basting regularly with the sauce. The pork is ready when the meat feels very tender when pierced with a fork.

Remove the meat and leave to rest for 10 minutes. The sauce, which should be biscuity in colour, will be unattractively lumpy, so vigorously whisk to break up the lumps or process in a food processor or blender until smooth. Reheat if necessary and season with salt and pepper. Separate the loin into 6 chops and serve with the sauce spooned over.

For lamb shanks braised in milk, replace the pork with 6 lamb shanks and cook as above, using 3 rosemary sprigs instead of the sage leaves. Add a generous grating of nutmeg to the sauce before whisking or blending away the lumps.

lamb cutlets with red pesto

Serves **4**
Preparation time **15 minutes**, plus marinating
Cooking time **4–6 minutes**

12 **lamb cutlets**, each approximately 100 g (3½ oz)
2 tablespoons **olive oil**
juice of ½ **lemon**
1 **garlic clove**, crushed
2 **rosemary sprigs**, roughly chopped
salt and **pepper**

Pesto
50 g (2 oz) **sunblush tomatoes**
75 g (3 oz) **bottled roasted peppers**
50 g (2 oz) **blanched almonds**
½ **red chilli**, halved and deseeded
2 **garlic cloves**, crushed
3 tablespoons freshly grated **Parmesan cheese**
3 tablespoons **extra virgin olive oil**

Put the cutlets in a bowl with the oil, lemon juice, garlic and rosemary and toss well to combine. Cover and leave to marinate in the refrigerator for at least 1 hour or up to overnight.

Meanwhile, for the pesto, put the tomatoes, peppers, almonds, chilli and garlic in a food processor and process to a paste. Stir in the Parmesan and oil and season with salt.

Season the marinated cutlets with salt and pepper. Heat a ridged griddle pan over a high heat until smoking hot, or preheat a gas barbecue to high or, if using a charcoal barbecue, get the coals to the stage where there are no more flames and the coals are covered with a thin layer of grey ash. Add the cutlets and cook for 2–3 minutes on each side, depending on whether you like your lamb pink in the centre or well done. Serve with the red pesto on the side.

For a steak sandwich with red pesto, replace the lamb with 500 g (1 lb) fillet steak. Marinate and cook as above, then slice. Meanwhile, make the red pesto as above. Cut 4 ciabatta rolls open and drizzle the inside with olive oil. Griddle or barbecue for a few seconds to char slightly. Put the beef slices in the rolls and top with wild rocket leaves, red pesto and a few slices of red onion.

devilled fillet steaks

Serves **4**
Preparation time **10 minutes**
Cooking time **10 minutes**

2 tablespoons **olive oil**
4 **fillet steaks**, about 175 g (6 oz) each
2 tablespoons **balsamic vinegar**
75 ml (3 fl oz) **full-bodied red wine**
4 tablespoons **beef stock**
2 **garlic cloves**, chopped
1 teaspoon crushed **fennel seeds**
1 tablespoon **sun-dried tomato purée**
½ teaspoon **crushed dried chillies**
salt and **pepper**

To garnish
chopped **flat leaf parsley**
wild rocket leaves (optional)

Heat the oil in a nonstick frying pan until smoking hot. Add the steaks and cook over a very high heat for about 2 minutes on each side, if you want your steaks to be medium rare. Remove to a plate, season with salt and pepper and keep warm in a low oven.

Pour the vinegar, wine and stock into the pan and boil for 30 seconds, scraping any sediment from the base of the pan. Add the garlic and fennel seeds and whisk in the sun-dried tomato purée and crushed chillies. Bring the sauce to the boil and boil fast to reduce until syrupy.

Transfer the steaks to warmed serving plates, pouring any collected meat juices into the sauce. Return the sauce to the boil, then season with salt and pepper.

Pour the sauce over the steaks and serve immediately, garnished with chopped parsley and wild rocket leaves, if liked. Slice the steaks before serving, if you wish.

For devilled chicken breasts, heat the oil and use to cook 4 skinned chicken breasts for 5 minutes on each side. Leaving the chicken in the pan, follow the recipe above, replacing the beef stock with 4 tablespoons chicken stock and using ½ teaspoon dried oregano instead of the fennel seeds.

rabbit in white wine & rosemary

Serves **4–6**
Preparation time **15 minutes**
Cooking time **2 hours**

25 g (1 oz) **butter**
3 tablespoons **olive oil**
1 **rabbit**, about 1.5 kg (3 lb), cut into joints (ask your butcher to do this for you)
2 **onions**, thinly sliced
1 small **celery stick**, finely diced
pinch of **crushed dried chillies**
3 large **rosemary sprigs**
1 **lemon**, quartered
12 **black olives**
350 ml (12 fl oz) **dry white wine**
250 ml (8 fl oz) **chicken stock**
salt

Melt half the butter with the oil in a large, flameproof casserole with a tight-fitting lid large enough to hold the rabbit in a single layer. Lightly season the rabbit with salt and add to the pan with the onions, celery, crushed chillies and rosemary. Cover and cook over a low heat for 1½ hours, turning the rabbit pieces every 30 minutes.

Uncover the pan, increase the heat to high and boil until most of the juices released by the rabbit during cooking have evaporated. Add the lemon and olives, stir well, then pour in the wine. Bring to the boil and boil for 2 minutes, for the alcohol to evaporate.

Pour in the stock and simmer, turning and basting the rabbit occasionally, for a further 10–12 minutes until you have a rich, syrupy sauce. Serve hot.

For chicken with olives & rosemary, replace the rabbit with 1 chicken, cut into 8 joints (ask your butcher to do this). Put the chicken with all the remaining ingredients above in a large roasting tin and roast in a preheated oven, 200°C (400°F), Gas Mark 6, for 1 hour, turning the chicken pieces occasionally, until the meat is tender and most of the juices have evaporated. Stir in 3 tablespoons double cream and serve immediately.

roast herbed pork belly

Serves **4–6**
Preparation time **15 minutes**, plus resting
Cooking time **1 hour 50 minutes**

10 **sage leaves**
2 large **rosemary sprigs**
3 **garlic cloves**, crushed
1 tablespoon **fennel seeds**
4 tablespoons **olive oil**
1 **boned pork belly joint**, about 1.25 kg (2½ lb)
salt and **pepper**

Roughly chop the sage and rosemary and combine with the garlic, fennel seeds and half the oil in a small bowl.

Place the pork on a chopping board, skin-side up, and score the rind at 2.5 cm (1 inch) intervals (the easiest way of doing this is with a Stanley knife). Turn the meat over, skin-side down, and season with salt and pepper. Rub the herb mixture all over the flesh. Roll the pork up and tie it tightly with string. Rub the skin all over with the remaining oil, then a generous amount of salt.

Roast in a preheated oven, 220°C (425°F), Gas Mark 7, for 20 minutes, then reduce the temperature to 160°C (325°F), Gas Mark 3, and roast for a further 1½ hours. Leave the meat to rest for 10 minutes before carving and serving. The Braised Black Cabbage & Borlotti on page 198 or the Braised Artichokes & Potatoes on page 186 would make great accompaniments for the pork.

For sausage & apricot stuffed pork, instead of the herb mixture, roughly chop 4 sage leaves and 6 ready-to-eat dried apricots, then stir into 150 g (5 oz) pork sausagemeat. Follow the recipe above from the second step onwards, spreading the sausagement mixture over the seasoned pork.

beef in red wine

Serves **4**
Preparation time **10 minutes**
Cooking time **2¼ hours**

875 g (1¾ lb) **brisket of beef**, cut into 5 cm (2 inch) pieces
1 **celery stick**
2 **bay leaves**
750 ml (1¼ pint) bottle **Barolo** or other full-bodied red wine
300 ml (½ pint) **beef** or **chicken stock**
2 **carrots**, cut at an angle into 3.5 cm (1½ inch) slices
20 **baby onions**, peeled but kept whole
salt and **pepper**

Season the beef with salt and pepper and put in a large, flameproof casserole with a tight-fitting lid. Add the celery and bay leaves, then pour in the wine and stock. Bring to the boil, then reduce the heat to a barely visible simmer and cook, covered, for 1½ hours, stirring occasionally.

Add the carrots and onions. Re-cover and simmer gently for a further 45 minutes, adding a little water if the sauce becomes too thick.

Remove the beef from the heat and serve accompanied by mashed potatoes or soft polenta.

For oxtail in red wine with tomatoes, replace the beef with 2 kg (4 lb) oxtail chunks. Cook as above, adding a 400 g (13 oz) can chopped tomatoes and reducing the red wine to 350 ml (12 fl oz). Simmer gently for 2½ hours. Oxtail releases a lot of fat, so ideally make the stew a day ahead, leave to cool completely, then refrigerate. Skim off the solidified layer of fat before reheating.

sausages & lentils in tomato sauce

Serves **4**
Preparation time **10 minutes**
Cooking time **1 hour 10 minutes**

3 tablespoons **olive oil**
8 **Italian pork sausages**
1 **onion**, roughly chopped
1 **celery stick**, roughly chopped
3 **garlic cloves**, crushed
200 ml (7 fl oz) **full-bodied red wine**
400 g (13 oz) can **chopped tomatoes**
1.2 litres (2 pints) **chicken stock**
1 **bay leaf**
1 **dried red chilli**
125 g (4 oz) **green lentils**
salt and **pepper**
extra virgin olive oil, for drizzling

Heat the oil in a large, heavy-based saucepan in which the sausages fit in a single layer. Add the sausages and cook over a medium heat for 10–12 minutes until golden brown all over. Remove and set aside.

Add the onion and celery to the pan and cook over a low heat for 8–10 minutes until softened. Stir in the garlic and cook for a further 2 minutes.

Increase the heat to high, pour in the wine and boil vigorously for 2 minutes, scraping any sediment from the base of the pan. Stir in the tomatoes, stock, bay leaf and chilli and bring to the boil. Add the lentils and return the sausages to the pan. Simmer gently for 40 minutes, or until the sausages and lentils are cooked through. Season with salt and pepper. Serve with a drizzle of extra virgin olive oil, accompanied by some crusty bread.

For cod & lentils in tomato sauce, omit the sausages and cook the other ingredients as above from the second step onwards, finally adding the lentils to the pan. Once cooked until tender, add 4 cod fillets, about 125 g (4 oz) each, to the pan and season with salt and pepper. Scatter with the grated rind of 1 lemon and 1 tablespoon chopped parsley, cover and cook over a low heat for 10–12 minutes until cooked through.

chicken milanese

Serves **4**
Preparation time **20 minutes**
Cooking time **10–25 minutes**

4 **boneless chicken breasts**, about 150–175 g (5–6 oz) each, skinned
100 g (3½ oz) **plain flour**
2 **eggs**, beaten
200 g (7 oz) **dry white breadcrumbs**
3 tablespoons **flat leaf parsley**, chopped
5 tablespoons **olive oil**
salt and **pepper**
lemon wedges, to serve

Lay the chicken breasts between 2 sheets of clingfilm and beat with a rolling pin until no more than 1 cm (½ inch) thick.

Put the flour, eggs and breadcrumbs in 3 separate dishes and season the flour and eggs with salt and pepper. Stir the chopped parsley into the breadcrumbs. Turn each chicken breast in the flour, then dip into the eggs and coat in the breadcrumbs.

Heat the oil in a frying pan over a high heat. Add the flattened chicken breasts, 1 or 2 at a time, and cook for 2–3 minutes on each side until golden. Remove with a slotted spoon and drain on kitchen paper. Serve with lemon wedges, accompanied by a crisp green salad.

For turkey Milanese, replace the chicken with 4 turkey breast steaks, about 150–175 g (5–6 oz) each, sliced 1 cm (½ inch) thick. For the coating, use 200 g (7 oz) fresh white breadcrumbs instead of the dry breadcrumbs and flavour with 2 crushed garlic cloves, 2 tablespoons chopped flat leaf parsley and 1 tablespoon chopped thyme. Follow the recipe above.

roast chicken with herbs & garlic

Serves **4**
Preparation time **10 minutes**
Cooking time **about 1 hour**

8 **garlic cloves**, unpeeled
4 large **thyme sprigs**
3 large **rosemary sprigs**
1 **organic** or **free-range chicken**, about 1.75 kg (3½ lb)
1 tablespoon **olive oil**
salt and **pepper**

Put the garlic cloves and half the herb sprigs in the body cavity of the chicken. Pat the chicken dry with kitchen paper and rub the oil all over the outside of the bird. Strip the leaves off the remaining herb sprigs and rub over the bird, with a little salt and pepper.

Place the chicken, breast-side up, in a roasting tin. Roast in a preheated oven, 220°C (425°F), Gas Mark 7, for 10 minutes. Turn the chicken over, breast-side down, reduce the oven temperature to 180°C (350°F), Gas Mark 4, and cook for a further 20 minutes. Finally, turn the chicken back to its original position and roast for another 25 minutes until the skin is crisp and golden. Check that the chicken is cooked by piercing the thigh with a knife. The juices should run clear, with no sign of pink. If not, cook for a further 10 minutes.

Transfer to a warmed serving plate and leave to rest for 5 minutes before serving with the pan juices.

For roast chicken with lemon & sage, cut a lemon in half, then cut 1 half into slices. Carefully lift the skin covering the breast meat and ease in the lemon slices. Put the other lemon half in the body cavity with 8 sage leaves, in place of the thyme and rosemary sprigs, and the garlic as above. Roast as above.

vegetables & legumes

aubergine & courgette parmigiana

Serves **6**
Preparation time **15 minutes**
Cooking time **45–50 minutes**

500 ml (17 fl oz) **passata**
handful of **basil leaves**, torn
2 **garlic cloves**, crushed
4 tablespoons **olive oil**
1 kg (2 lb) **aubergines**, cut lengthways into 1 cm (½ inch) slices
500 g (1 lb) **courgettes**, cut lengthways into 1 cm (½ inch) slices
300 g (10 oz) **mozzarella cheese** (drained weight), chopped
100 g (3½ oz) **Parmesan cheese**, freshly grated
salt and **pepper**

Combine the passata, basil and garlic in a bowl, season with salt and pepper and stir in half the oil.

Toss the aubergines and courgettes in the remaining oil to coat. Heat a ridged griddle pan over a high heat until smoking hot. Add the vegetables, in batches, and cook for 2–3 minutes on each side until tender all the way through.

Spoon a little of the passata mixture on to the base of a deep baking dish, about 30 x 20 cm (12 x 8 inches). Cover with a layer of mixed aubergines and courgettes, then scatter with some of the mozzarella. Spoon over 4 tablespoons of the passata mixture and scatter with Parmesan. Continue layering in this way until all the ingredients are used up, finishing with a layer of passata mixture and Parmesan.

Bake in a preheated oven, 180°C (350°F), Gas Mark 4, for 25–30 minutes, or until golden and bubbly.

For fennel & olive parmigiana, replace the aubergines and courgettes with 4 fennel bulbs, cut lengthways into 1 cm (½ inch) slices and 1 large onion, sliced into rings. Griddle and layer with the passata mixture and cheese as above, then top the final layer with a scattering of 15 pitted black olives. Bake as above.

grilled radicchio, fontina & speck

Serves **4**
Preparation time **10 minutes**
Cooking time **15 minutes**

4 **radicchi di treviso** or
  2 **round radicchi**
2 tablespoons **olive oil**
8 slices of **speck**
75 g (3 oz) **Fontina cheese**,
  thinly sliced
salt and **pepper**

Cut radicchio di treviso in half lengthways. If using round radicchio, cut into quarters. Brush all sides of the radicchio with the oil, then season with salt and pepper. Arrange on a baking sheet and cook under a preheated medium grill, about 12 cm (5 inches) from the heat source, for 10 minutes, until slightly softened. The leaves will darken in colour, but they should not char, so reduce the heat or increase the distance between the radicchio and the heat source if necessary.

Drape each piece of radicchio with a slice of speck, then top with the Fontina. Grill for a further 2 minutes until the cheese has melted and serve.

For grilled radicchio with walnut vinaigrette, first make the vinaigrette by whisking together 1 tablespoon grainy mustard, 3 tablespoons walnut oil and 2 tablespoons groundnut oil in a bowl. Stir in 2 tablespoons roughly chopped walnuts and season with salt and pepper. Grill the radicchio as above, omitting the speck and cheese topping. Transfer to a serving bowl, spoon over the vinaigrette and serve warm.

cannellini with sage & tomato

Serves **4**
Preparation time **10–15 minutes**, plus soaking (optional)
Cooking time **15 minutes** for canned beans; **45 minutes** for fresh; **1¾ hours** for dried

250 g (8 oz) shelled **fresh cannellini beans**, or 200 g (7 oz) **dried cannellini beans**, soaked in cold water overnight, drained and rinsed, or 2 x 400 g (13 oz) cans **cannellini beans**, drained and rinsed
1 **bay leaf** (optional)
2 **garlic cloves**, unpeeled, or 1 garlic clove, chopped
2 teaspoons **olive oil**
1 **red onion**, thinly sliced
5 **sage leaves**, roughly chopped
pinch of **crushed dried chillies**
2 **tomatoes**, skinned and chopped
salt
extra virgin olive oil, for drizzling (optional)

Put the fresh beans, if using, into a saucepan, pour in enough cold water to cover by about 5 cm (2 inches) and add the bay leaf, and garlic cloves. Bring to the boil and skim off any scum that rises to the surface. Reduce the heat to a simmer and cook, uncovered, for 25–30 minutes, or until tender. Drain, reserving the garlic cloves. If using presoaked dried beans, cook as for the fresh beans, but they will take about 1½ hours to become tender. The canned beans are ready to use.

Heat the oil in a large, heavy-based frying pan over a low heat. Add the onion, sage and crushed chillies and cook, stirring occasionally, for 10 minutes until the onion is softened. If you cooked the beans from scratch, squeeze the garlic flesh out of the skins into the pan. If using canned beans, simply add the chopped garlic to the pan. Cook, stirring, for 1 minute, then add the beans and the tomatoes. Season with salt and cook, stirring, for 3–5 minutes. Serve drizzled with a little extra virgin olive oil, if liked.

For cannellini with pancetta & rosemary, prepare the beans following the first stage of the recipe above. Fry the onions and chilli in olive oil as above, omitting the sage and adding 75 g (3 oz) cubed pancetta and 1 large sprig of rosemary. Complete the recipe as above.

braised artichokes & potatoes

Serves **4**
Preparation time **30 minutes**
Cooking time **1 hour**

6 **baby globe artichokes**
juice of 1 **lemon**
4 tablespoons **olive oil**
2 **shallots**, thinly sliced
1 **garlic clove**, finely chopped
500 g (1 lb) **potatoes**, peeled and cut into 3.5 cm (1½ inch) chunks
100 g (3½ oz) shelled **fresh** or **frozen peas**
handful of **flat leaf parsley**, roughly chopped
salt and **pepper**

Trim the stalks of the artichokes, leaving about 3 cm (1¼ inches). Pull off and discard the tough outer leaves, exposing the paler tender leaves, then cut off their tips. Using a potato peeler, peel the stalk and dark green base until you see the lighter, yellowy flesh. Halve the artichokes and scoop out the hairy choke with a teaspoon and discard. Put in a bowl of cold water with the lemon juice to prevent discolouring.

Heat the oil in a large, heavy-based saucepan with a tight-fitting lid just large enough to hold the artichokes and potatoes in a single layer. Add the shallots and cook over a medium heat for 8–10 minutes until softened and translucent. Add the garlic and cook, stirring, for 1 minute. Toss in the drained artichokes, potatoes and salt and pepper.

Pour in enough water to come a quarter of the way up the vegetables. Bring to the boil, then reduce to a slow simmer. Cover with greaseproof paper and the lid. Cook for 45 minutes. Stir in the peas and parsley and cook for a further 5 minutes, or until the artichokes and potatoes are tender.

For braised courgettes, peas & prosciutto, omit the artichokes and potatoes. Cut 75 g (3 oz) prosciutto into thin strips and cook with the shallots as above. Once the garlic has cooked for 1 minute, stir in 2 courgettes, cut into 1 cm (½ inch) slices. Complete the recipe as above, but using 2 tablespoons chopped mint instead of the parsley.

sicilian caponata

Serves **4**
Preparation time **15 minutes**, plus standing
Cooking time **30 minutes**

100 ml (3½ fl oz) **olive oil**
2 **aubergines**, cut into 3.5 cm (1½ inch) cubes
1 large **onion**, coarsely chopped
3 **celery sticks**, sliced
50 g (2 oz) **pine nuts**
2 **garlic cloves**, chopped
400 g (13 oz) can **plum tomatoes**, drained and roughly chopped
2 tablespoons **capers in brine**, rinsed
50 g (2 oz) **pitted green olives**
3 tablespoons **red wine vinegar**
1 tablespoon **caster sugar**
6 **basil leaves**
salt and **pepper**

Heat the oil in a large frying pan over a high heat until the oil begins to shimmer. Add the aubergines, in batches, and cook, stirring frequently, for 5–6 minutes until they are golden and tender. Use a slotted spoon to transfer to a bowl.

Pour away all but 2 tablespoons oil from the pan. Add the onion, celery and pine nuts and cook over a low heat for 10 minutes until the vegetables are softened and lightly golden. Return the aubergines to the pan and stir in the remaining ingredients, except for the basil. Season with salt and pepper.

Bring the pan to the boil, then reduce the heat and simmer for 5 minutes. Stir in the basil. Remove from the heat and leave to stand for at least 15 minutes to allow the flavours to mingle. Serve warm or cold, as an antipasto, side dish or as a vegetarian main course, with some bread on the side.

For potato & pepper caponata, peel and cut 500 g (1 lb) potatoes into 3.5 cm (1½ inch) cubes. Cook in a saucepan of salted boiling water until tender, then drain. Omit the aubergine. Reduce the oil to 4 tablespoons and heat in a frying pan. Add the onion, celery and pine nuts with 2 red peppers, cored, deseeded and cut into large chunks, and cook as above. Toss in the potatoes and the remaining ingredients as above, but using black olives in place of the green. Season with salt and pepper, then follow the final step above to complete.

squash with mascarpone & sage

Serves **4**
Preparation time **15 minutes**
Cooking time **1 hour 10 minutes**

2 small **acorn squash**, each about 500 g (1 lb)
2 tablespoons **olive oil**
125 g (4 oz) piece **smoked pancetta**, diced
2 **garlic cloves**, crushed
2 tablespoons chopped **sage**, plus extra, to garnish
175 g (6 oz) **mascarpone cheese**
4 **sun-dried tomatoes** in oil, drained and chopped
2 tablespoons freshly grated **Parmesan cheese**
salt and **pepper**

To serve
grilled **bread**
green salad

Cut the squash in half lengthways and carefully scoop out the seeds. Season the shells lightly with salt and pepper and place, cut side up, in a roasting tin. Drizzle with a little of the oil and bake in a preheated oven, 200°C (400°F), Gas Mark 6, for 45 minutes.

Dry-fry the pancetta for about 5 minutes, until it is golden and has released its fat. Lower the heat, add the remaining oil and gently fry the garlic and sage for a further 4–5 minutes, until the garlic is softened.

Remove the squash from the oven and fill the hollows with the pancetta mixture. Spoon in the mascarpone and scatter over the sun-dried tomatoes and Parmesan. Return to the oven for 15–20 minutes, until bubbling and golden. Garnish with sage leaves and serve with some grilled bread and a crisp green salad.

For aubergines with pancetta & sage, cut 2 aubergines in half lengthways and roast instead of the squash, as above. Follow step 2 and stir 3 tablespoons each fresh white breadcrumbs and grated Parmesan into the pancetta mixture. Use to top the aubergines and bake for a further 15 minutes.

garlicky potatoes with tomatoes

Serves **4**
Preparation time **10 minutes**
Cooking time **1 hour**

625 g (1¼ lb) **potatoes**, unpeeled
2 **onions**, thickly sliced
1 **garlic bulb**, broken into cloves
200 g (7 oz) **cherry tomatoes**, on the vine
3 tablespoons **extra virgin olive oil**
150 ml (¼ pint) **dry white wine**
1 teaspoon **dried oregano**
pared **rind** of 1 small **orange**
salt and **pepper**

Cut the potatoes in half lengthways, then each half into 3 wedges. Put in a large roasting tin with all the remaining ingredients, season with salt and pepper and stir well to combine thoroughly.

Roast in a preheated oven, 200°C (400°F), Gas Mark 6, for 1 hour, or until the potatoes are cooked through. Stir the vegetables in the tin a couple of times during cooking. If the liquid dries out so much that the tomatoes and onions begin to stick to the base, add a little hot water to stop them burning.

For potatoes with red peppers & olives, prepare the potatoes and put in the roasting tin with the remaining ingredients as above, but omit the garlic, tomatoes and orange rind. Toss in 2 red peppers, cored, deseeded and cut into 2.5 cm (1 inch) strips, season with salt and pepper and roast as above for 50 minutes. Stir in 50 g (2 oz) pitted black olives and roast for a further 10 minutes. Stir in a handful of basil leaves.

peperonata

Serves **4**
Preparation time **10 minutes**, plus preparing the peppers
Cooking time **45 minutes**

2 large **red peppers**, grilled, skinned, cored and deseeded (see page 46)
2 large **yellow peppers**, grilled, skinned, cored and deseeded (see page 46)
2 teaspoons **olive oil**
1 small **onion**, finely chopped
2 **garlic cloves**, finely chopped
400 g (13 oz) can **plum tomatoes**, roughly chopped
6 large **basil leaves**, torn
extra virgin olive oil, for drizzling (optional)
salt

Cut the peppers into wide strips and set aside.

Heat the oil in a heavy-based saucepan over a low heat. Add the onion and cook, stirring occasionally, for 10 minutes. Add the garlic and cook, stirring, for 1 minute. Add the tomatoes and their juice and the pepper strips. Season with salt and bring to the boil. Reduce the heat to a gentle simmer and cook, stirring occasionally, for 25 minutes.

Stir the basil into the pan and cook for a further 5–10 minutes until the sauce has reduced. Drizzle with extra virgin olive oil before serving, if liked. Serve immediately as a side dish, or spoon over soft polenta or stir into pasta. Alternatively, serve cold as an antipasto.

For caper & lemon peperonata, follow the recipe as above also adding 2 tablespoons capers and the grated zest of 1 lemon to the pan with the basil.

spinach & pea frittata

Serves **4**
Preparation time **10 minutes**
Cooking time **25 minutes**

1 tablespoon **olive oil**
1 **onion**, thinly sliced
150 g (5 oz) **baby spinach**
125 g (4 oz) shelled **fresh** or **frozen peas**
6 **eggs**
salt and **pepper**

Heat the oil in a heavy-based, ovenproof, nonstick 23 cm (9 inch) frying pan over a low heat. Add the onion and cook for 6–8 minutes until softened, then stir in the spinach and peas and cook for a further 2 minutes, or until any moisture released by the spinach has evaporated.

Beat the eggs in a bowl and season lightly with salt and pepper. Stir in the cooked vegetables, then pour the mixture into the pan and quickly arrange the vegetables so that they are evenly dispersed. Cook over a low heat for 8–10 minutes, or until all but the top of the frittata is set.

Transfer the pan to a preheated very hot grill and cook about 10 cm (4 inches) from the heat source until the top is set but not coloured. Give the pan a shake to loosen the frittata, then transfer to a plate to cool. Serve slightly warm or at room temperature, accompanied by a green salad.

For courgette, pea & cheese frittata, follow the first step above, but replace the spinach with 1 large courgette, coarsely grated. Add 4 tablespoons freshly grated Parmesan cheese and 100 g (3½ oz) cubed mozzarella cheese to the raw egg mixture with the vegetables and cook as above.

braised black cabbage & borlotti

Serves **4**
Preparation time **10 minutes**
Cooking time **30 minutes**

1.5 kg (3 lb) **cavolo nero (black cabbage)**
3 tablespoons **olive oil**
2 **garlic cloves**, thinly sliced
¼ teaspoon **crushed dried chillies**
400 g (13 oz) can **borlotti beans**, drained and rinsed
salt

Remove the thick stalks of the cabbage by holding the stems with one hand and using the other hand to strip away the leaves. Discard the stalks. Cook the leaves in a saucepan of boiling water for 15 minutes until just tender, then drain thoroughly.

Heat the oil in a large frying pan over a low heat. Add the garlic, crushed chillies and borlotti beans and cook for 5 minutes, then stir in the cooked cabbage. Season with salt and cook, stirring, for 6–8 minutes until the cabbage has completely wilted and absorbed the flavours. Serve immediately.

For spinach with pine nuts, follow the recipe above from the second step onwards, replacing the borlotti beans with 50 g (2 oz) pine nuts. Use 500 g (1 lb) baby spinach, instead of the cabbage, toss into the pan raw and cook, stirring, for 2–3 minutes until wilted. Stir a light grating of nutmeg into the cooked spinach before serving.

potato & green bean bake

Serves **4**
Preparation time **10 minutes**
Cooking time **45 minutes**

500 g (1 lb) **floury potatoes**, peeled and cut into large chunks
300 g (10 oz) **green beans**, trimmed and halved
2 **garlic cloves**, finely chopped
handful of **basil leaves**, torn
100 g (3½ oz) **Parmesan cheese**, freshly grated
200 g (7 oz) **ricotta cheese**
3 **eggs**, lightly beaten
100 g (3½ oz) **fresh white breadcrumbs**
2 tablespoons **olive oil**, plus extra for oiling
salt and **pepper**

Simmer the potatoes in a saucepan of salted boiling water for 10 minutes, then add the beans and cook for a further 3–4 minutes until the potatoes are cooked through and the beans are just tender. Drain, return to the pan and mash to a lumpy purée.

Stir the garlic, basil, cheeses and eggs into the vegetable purée and season with salt and pepper.

Sprinkle an oiled cake tin or ovenproof dish with a thin layer of the breadcrumbs. Pile in the vegetable mash, sprinkle with the remaining breadcrumbs and drizzle with the oil. Bake in a preheated oven, 200°C (400°F), Gas Mark 6, for 25–30 minutes until the topping is crisp and golden.

For potato, olive & sunblush tomato bake, cook the potatoes and mash as above, but omit the beans. Stir the garlic, eggs and cheeses into the mash as above together with 50 g (2 oz) roughly chopped pitted black olives and 8 roughly chopped sunblush tomatoes, replacing the basil with ½ teaspoon dried oregano. Follow the final step above to complete.

desserts

lemon panna cotta & raspberries

Serves **6**
Preparation time **10 minutes**, plus chilling and marinating
Cooking time **5 minutes**

600 ml (1 pint) **double cream**
100 g (3½ oz) **caster sugar**
pared **rind** of 2 **lemons**
1 **vanilla pod**, split lengthways and seeds removed
350 ml (12 fl oz) **milk**
3 teaspoons **powdered gelatine**
100 g (3½ oz) **fresh raspberries**
5 **mint leaves**, roughly chopped
3 tablespoons **grappa**

Put the cream, sugar, lemon rind and vanilla seeds in a saucepan. Bring to the boil over a low heat, then remove from the heat and leave to infuse for 5 minutes.

Meanwhile, bring the milk to the boil in a separate saucepan. Remove from the heat and carefully sprinkle with the gelatine, in as thin and even a layer as you can manage. Leave to stand for 2–3 minutes until the gelatine no longer looks dry, then stir to dissolve.

Strain the infused cream through a sieve into the milk and pour the mixture into 6 x 175 ml (6 fl oz) dariole moulds. Cover each with clingfilm and chill for at least 5 hours until set. It will keep for up to 3 days in the refrigerator.

Combine the raspberries, mint and grappa in a bowl. Cover and leave to marinate at room temperature for 30 minutes and up to 4 hours.

Unmould the panna cotta by carefully dipping the base and sides of the moulds in warm water for a few seconds. Invert on to individual serving plates and serve with the marinated raspberries.

For coffee-cream liqueur panna cotta, omit the lemon rind and the first step above. Dissolve the gelatine in the milk, as in the second step, then stir in 300 ml (½ pint) each coffee-flavoured cream liqueur and double cream. Pour into the dariole moulds and chill as above. Instead of the marinated raspberries, serve with the coffee sauce on page 216.

apricot jam tart

Serves **6–8**
Preparation time **20 minutes**, plus chilling
Cooking time **20–25 minutes**

275 g (9 oz) **plain flour**, plus extra for dusting
75 g (3 oz) **caster sugar**
125 g (4 oz) **unsalted butter**, diced
1 **egg** and 1 **egg yolk**, lightly beaten
250 g (8 oz) **low-sugar apricot jam**
icing sugar, for dusting

Put the flour and caster sugar in a bowl, add the butter and rub in with your fingertips until the mixture resembles coarse breadcrumbs. Gradually mix in enough of the eggs to bring the pastry together. Knead very lightly into a dough. Cover with clingfilm and chill for 30–45 minutes.

Roll two-thirds of the pastry out on a lightly floured work surface. Use to line a shallow, 23 cm (9 inch) fluted tart tin, then fill with the jam. Roll the remaining pastry out to a thickness of about 5 mm (¼ inch), then cut strips about 1 cm (½ inch) wide. Lightly brush the rim of the pastry case with water. Arrange the pastry strips in a lattice pattern over the tart. Chill for 20 minutes until firm.

Bake on a baking sheet in a preheated oven, 200°C (400°F), Gas Mark 6, for 20–25 minutes until the pastry is firm and golden. Leave to cool on a wire rack, then remove from the tin and serve with a generous dusting of icing sugar. The tart will keep in an airtight container for up to 2 days.

For chocolate & raspberry jam tart, reduce the quantity of flour in the pastry to 200 g (7 oz) and stir in 75 g (3 oz) cocoa powder with the sugar before rubbing in the butter. Use the pastry to line the tin as above, then fill with 250 g (8 oz) low-sugar raspberry jam instead of the apricot. Finish the tart and bake as above.

chocolate & hazelnut parfaits

Serves **6**
Preparation time **20 minutes**, plus cooling and freezing
Cooking time **5–10 minutes**

125 g (4 oz) **blanched hazelnuts**
125 g (4 oz) **plain dark chocolate with 70% cocoa solids**, broken into pieces, plus extra **chocolate curls** to decorate
600 ml (1 pint) **double cream**
2 **eggs**, separated
175 g (6 oz) **icing sugar**
cocoa powder, to decorate

Spread the hazelnuts out on a baking sheet and toast in a preheated oven, 160°C (325°F), Gas Mark 3, for 5–10 minutes until golden. Leave to cool completely, then grind very finely.

Put the chocolate in a heatproof bowl set over a saucepan of hot water and leave to melt. Whip the cream in a bowl until it holds its shape, then fold in the nuts. Whisk the egg yolks in a large bowl with 2 tablespoons of the icing sugar until pale and creamy. Whisk the egg whites in a separate bowl until soft peaks form, then add the remaining icing sugar, spoonful by spoonful, whisking well after each addition, until the mixture is very thick.

Stir the melted chocolate into the egg yolk mixture. Fold in the cream mixture, then the meringue mixture. Turn into 6 x 175 ml (6 fl oz) moulds and freeze for 6 hours until firm.

Transfer to the refrigerator for 10 minutes before serving to soften slightly. Decorate with chocolate curls and dust with cocoa powder. Serve with dessert biscuits.

For chocolate, almond & prune parfaits, replace the hazelnuts with blanched almonds and prepare as above. Roughly chop 6 prunes and soak in 3 tablespoons of grappa for 30 minutes. Follow the recipe above, folding in the prunes just before turning the mixture into the moulds. Complete as above.

lemon & ricotta tart

Serves **8–10**
Preparation time **15 minutes**, plus chilling
Cooking time **50–55 minutes**

350 g (11½ oz) **ready-made sweet shortcrust pastry**
plain flour, for dusting
4 **eggs**
100 g (3½ oz) **caster sugar**
350 g (11½ oz) **ricotta cheese**
400 ml (14 fl oz) **double cream**
rind and **juice** of 3 **lemons**
fresh berries, to decorate

Roll the pastry out on a lightly floured work surface. Use to line a 23 cm (9 inch) fluted tart tin, then chill for 10 minutes. Line the pastry case with greaseproof paper and fill with baking beans.

Bake the pastry case in a preheated oven, 180°C (350°F), Gas Mark 4, for 10 minutes. Remove the baking beans and paper and bake for a further 5 minutes until golden.

Whisk the remaining ingredients together in a bowl and use to fill the pastry case. Reduce the oven temperature to 150°C (300°F), Gas Mark 2, and bake the tart for 35–40 minutes until just set. Serve with fresh berries, such as strawberries and blueberries, and a generous dusting of icing sugar.

For chocolate & ricotta tart, make and bake the pastry case as above. Then make the filling as above, but omit the lemon rind and juice and increase the double cream to 500 ml (17 fl oz). Stir in 100 g (3½ oz) roughly chopped plain dark chocolate. Use to fill the pastry case and bake as above.

pear & almond cake

Serves **8**
Preparation time **20 minutes**
Cooking time **35 minutes**

- 125 g (4 oz) **unsalted butter**, softened, plus extra for greasing
- 125 g (4 oz) **caster sugar**
- 2 large **eggs**, beaten
- 50 g (2 oz) **plain flour**, sifted
- 100 g (3½ oz) **ground almonds**
- ½ teaspoon **baking powder**
- 3 **ripe pears**, peeled, halved and cored
- 50 g (2 oz) **flaked almonds**
- **icing sugar**, for dusting

Beat the butter and caster sugar together in a bowl until pale and fluffy. Add the eggs, a little at a time, beating well after each addition. If the mixture starts to curdle, add 1 tablespoon of the flour. Fold in the flour, ground almonds and baking powder using a large metal spoon and tip into a greased 20 cm (8 inch) spring form cake tin and use a palette knife to even out the mixture.

Arrange the pear halves over the top of the cake and bake in a preheated oven, 190°C (375°F), Gas Mark 5, for 25 minutes. Sprinkle the flaked almonds over the top and return to the oven for a further 10 minutes. The cake is ready when a skewer inserted into the centre of the cake comes out clean.

Leave the cake to cool in the tin, then carefully remove the ring and base. Dust with icing sugar before serving with Mascarpone, Marsala & Orange Cream (see below), if liked.

For mascarpone, Marsala & orange cream, to serve as an accompaniment, whisk the grated rind of 1 orange and 2 tablespoons of its juice in a bowl with 2 tablespoons sweet Marsala and 100 g (3½ oz) mascarpone cheese. Sweeten with icing sugar to taste.

caramel panna cotta & apricots

Serves **4**
Preparation time **30 minutes**, plus standing, cooling and chilling
Cooking time **15 minutes**

600 ml (1 pint) **double cream**
125 g (4 oz) **caster sugar**
1 **vanilla pod**, split lengthways
75 ml (3 fl oz) **granulated sugar**
2 tablespoons **water**
4 tablespoons **milk**
1 tablespoon **powdered gelatine**

Apricots
8 **ripe apricots**, halved, stoned and cut into thirds
150 ml (¼ pint) **water**
75 g (3 oz) **caster sugar**
1 **vanilla pod**, split lengthways

Put the cream, caster sugar and vanilla pod in a saucepan and heat until just below boiling point, stirring occasionally. Remove from the heat and leave to infuse for 20 minutes.

Meanwhile, heat the granulated sugar in the measurement water in a heavy-based saucepan until it has dissolved, then boil until the syrup turns to a golden caramel. Quickly pour into 4 x 150 ml (¼ pint) ramekins or small moulds. Set on a tray and leave to harden.

Pour the milk into a small saucepan and sprinkle on the gelatine. Warm over a low heat until the gelatine dissolves. Stir into the infused cream mixture. Bring to the boil, then immediately remove from the heat and strain through a sieve into a jug. Pour into the ramekins or moulds. Leave to cool, then for at least 5 hours, until set.

Put the apricots in a small saucepan with the measurement water, sugar and vanilla pod. Bring slowly to the boil, then cover and simmer gently for 5–8 minutes until just tender. Leave to cool, then remove the vanilla pod, cover and chill.

Carefully loosen the panna cottas and turn out on to individual serving plates. Serve with the apricots.

For citrus peel panna cotta, scatter 50 g (2 oz) chopped citrus peel over the set caramel, before filling the ramekins or moulds with the panna cotta mixture. Omit the apricot sauce and serve instead with a drizzle of Limoncello liqueur.

zabaglione semifreddo with coffee

Serves **6**
Preparation time **15 minutes**, plus freezing
Cooking time **10 minutes**

6 **egg yolks**
100 g (3½ oz) **caster sugar**
100 ml (3½ fl oz) **sweet Marsala**
300 ml (½ pint) **double cream**
30 **sponge fingers**

Coffee sauce
200 ml (7 fl oz) **cold espresso coffee**
100 g (3½ oz) **granulated sugar**
3 tablespoons **coffee-flavoured liqueur**

Whisk the egg yolks with the caster sugar in a heatproof bowl set over a saucepan of gently simmering water until the sugar has melted. Add the Marsala and continue whisking for another 6–8 minutes, or until the mixture has thickened and holds its shape.

Whip the cream in a bowl until soft peaks form. Gently fold in the egg mixture. Roughly break the sponge fingers, then fold into the zabaglione. Tip into a 1 kg (2 lb) loaf tin lined with clingfilm. Cover with clingfilm and freeze for at least 6 hours or overnight until set.

Make the coffee sauce. Heat the coffee in a small saucepan, add the granulated sugar and stir until melted. Add the liqueur and boil vigorously until the sauce becomes thick and syrupy.

Turn the semifreddo out on to a serving plate and spoon over the sauce, which can be warm or at room temperature. Serve cut into slices.

For individual zabaglione semifreddos with raspberry sauce, make the zabaglione mixture as above and set in 6 dariole moulds lined with clingfilm. In place of the coffee sauce, heat 150 g (5 oz) raspberries in a small saucepan with 1 tablespoon caster sugar and 50 ml (2 fl oz) apple juice. Bring to the boil, then simmer gently for 2 minutes. Crush the berries with the back of a fork and squeeze in the juice of ½ lemon. Invert the semifreddos on to individual plates and serve with the sauce.

almond biscuits

Makes about **14**
Preparation time **20 minutes**
Cooking time **10 minutes**

150 g (5 oz) **ground almonds**
1 tablespoon **plain flour**
175 g (6 oz) **caster sugar**, plus extra for coating
½ teaspoon **baking powder**
1 **egg white**
½ teaspoon **vanilla extract**

Combine the almonds, flour, sugar and baking powder in a large bowl. Beat the egg white in a separate bowl until it holds its shape and has a consistency resembling shaving foam. Fold into the almond mixture. Add the vanilla extract and stir to combine thoroughly.

Dust a work surface with sugar. Roll 1 tablespoon of the biscuit dough in the palm of your hands to make a sausage shape about 6 cm (2½ inches) long. Roll in the sugar, then place on a baking sheet lined with baking parchment. Repeat with the remaining dough to make about 14 biscuits. Make sure you leave plenty of space between each biscuit, as they spread during cooking.

Bake the biscuits in a preheated oven, 200°C (400°F), Gas Mark 6, for 10 minutes until lightly golden.

For candied fruit & sultana biscuits, prepare the biscuit dough as above, but reduce the caster sugar to 150 g (5 oz) and stir in 2 tablespoons chopped candied peel, and 2 tablespoons sultanas with the vanilla extract. Shape into rolls, coat and bake as above.

chocolate sorbet

Makes about **900 ml (1½ pints)**
Preparation time **15 minutes**, plus chilling and freezing
Cooking time **10 minutes**

600 ml (1 pint) **water**
150 g (5 oz) **soft dark brown sugar**
200 g (7 oz) **granulated sugar**
65 g (2½ oz) **unsweetened cocoa powder**
25 g (1 oz) **plain dark chocolate with 70% cocoa solids**, finely chopped
2½ teaspoons **vanilla extract**
1 teaspoon **instant espresso coffee powder**

Put the measurement water, sugars and cocoa powder in a saucepan and mix together. Heat gently, stirring until the sugar has dissolved. Increase the heat to bring the mixture to a boil, then reduce to a simmer for 8 minutes.

Remove the pan from the heat and stir in the chocolate, vanilla extract and espresso powder until thoroughly dissolved. Pour into a bowl and cool over ice or leave to cool and chill.

Freeze in an ice-cream machine according to the manufacturer's instructions. Serve immediately or transfer to a chilled plastic freezerproof container and store in the freezer for up to 1 month. If you are using the sorbet straight from the freezer, transfer to the refrigerator 20 minutes before serving to soften slightly.

For rum & chocolate-chip sorbet, replace the vanilla extract with 3 tablespoons dark rum. Stir 75 g (3 oz) chopped plain dark chocolate into the ice-cream mixture before churning.

classic tiramisu

Serves **4**
Preparation time **20 minutes**, plus chilling

3 **eggs**, separated
125 g (4 oz) **caster sugar**
250 g (8 oz) **mascarpone cheese**
200 ml (7 fl oz) **cold espresso coffee**
4 tablespoons **sweet Marsala**
32–34 **sponge fingers**
75 g (3 oz) **plain dark chocolate**, grated

Whisk the egg yolks and sugar in a bowl with a hand-held electric whisk until light, airy and the beaters leave a trail when lifted. Put the mascarpone in a large bowl and beat in one-third of the egg mixture until smooth, then fold in the remaining egg mixture. Beat the egg whites in a separate bowl until they hold their shape and have a consistency resembling shaving foam. Fold into the mascarpone mixture.

Pour the coffee and Marsala into a shallow bowl and dip in the sponge fingers until soaked on both sides but not all the way through. Arrange a layer of tightly packed biscuits in four 10 cm (4 inch) bowls. Spread with half the mascarpone mixture, then top with a second layer of soaked sponge fingers. Use the remaining mascarpone mixture to cover the sponge fingers. Cover with clingfilm and chill for at least 3 hours or up to overnight.

Just before serving, remove the tiramisu from the refrigerator and dust with the grated chocolate.

For blackberry & lemon tiramisu, make the mascarpone mixture as above, but add 125 g (4 oz) crushed blackberries and the finely grated rind of 1 lemon at the end of the first step. Complete the recipe as above, but decorate the top with blackberries before dusting with grated chocolate.

panettone

Serves **8**
Preparation time **25 minutes**, plus rising
Cooking time **55 minutes**

1 tablespoon **active dried yeast**
150 ml (¼ pint) warm **milk**
about 500 g (1 lb) **strong plain white flour**, plus extra for dusting
2 teaspoons **salt**
1 **egg**, plus 4 **egg yolks**
75 g (3 oz) **caster sugar**
finely grated rind of 1 **lemon**
finely grated rind of 1 **orange**
175 g (6 oz) **unsalted butter**, softened
50 g (2 oz) chopped **candied orange** and **lemon peel**
125 g (4 oz) **raisins**

Line a deep 16 cm (6½ inch) cake tin with a double strip of nonstick baking parchment which projects 12.5 cm (5 inches) above the rim. Also line the bottom of the tin with baking parchment.

Dissolve the yeast in 4 tablespoons of the warm milk in a large bowl. Cover the bowl with a tea towel and leave in a warm place for 10 minutes until frothy. Stir in 125 g (4 oz) of the flour and the remaining warm milk. Cover and leave to rise for 30 minutes.

Sift the remaining flour and salt on to the yeast mixture. Beat together the egg and egg yolks. Make a well in the flour and add the beaten eggs, sugar and grated lemon and orange rind and mix to an elastic dough. Add more flour if necessary, but keep the dough quite soft.

Work in the softened butter. Cover and leave to rise for 2–4 hours until doubled in size. Meanwhile, chop the candied peel. Knock the dough down and knead in the fruit.

Place the dough in the tin, cut a cross on the top with a very sharp knife, cover and leave to rise to 2.5 cm (1 inch) above the top of the tin. Bake in a preheated oven, 200°C (400°F), Gas Mark 6 for 15 minutes then lower the heat to 180°C (350°F), Gas Mark 4 and bake for about 40 minutes until well risen and golden. Leave to cool in the tin for 10 minutes then transfer to a wire rack to cool completely.

For chocolate & nut panettone, follow the recipe above, replacing the candied peel and raisins with 150g (5 oz) roughly chopped dark chocolate and 100 g (3½ oz) chopped toasted almonds or hazelnuts.

hazelnut chocolate ice cream

Serves **4**
Preparation time **10 minutes**, plus freezing
Cooking time **5 minutes**

150 g (5 oz) **blanched hazelnuts**
350 g (11½ oz) **hazelnut and chocolate spread**
400 g (13 oz) can **evaporated milk**

Roughly crush the hazelnuts, then toast in a frying pan over a low heat until lightly golden. Leave to cool.

Tip the spread into a bowl and stir in a quarter of the evaporated milk until you have a smooth mixture. Stir in the remaining evaporated milk, then fold in 100 g (3½ oz) toasted hazelnuts.

Churn in an ice-cream machine according to the manufacturer's instructions. Transfer to a plastic freezerproof container and freeze.

Alternatively, freeze the mixture in a shallow container or tray for 2 hours until half-frozen, then tip into a bowl and whisk thoroughly to break up any ice crystals that may have formed. Return the mixture to the container and the freezer. Repeat the process at hourly intervals until the mixture is smooth and almost set. Finally, transfer the ice cream to a plastic freezerproof container and freeze until firm.

Remove the ice cream from the freezer 10 minutes before serving to soften slightly; it is best eaten within 48 hours. Scatter with the remaining hazelnuts and serve.

For speedy chunky chocolate ice cream, tip a 400 g (13 oz) tub good-quality chocolate ice cream into a bowl and leave to soften slightly. Lightly crush 75 g (3 oz) chocolate wafer biscuits and vigorously stir into the ice cream. Transfer to a plastic freezerproof container and freeze. Remove from the freezer and leave to soften slightly as above before serving.

sweet pastry ribbons

Makes about **35 ribbons**
Preparation time **25 minutes**
Cooking time **10 minutes**

1 **egg**
pinch of **salt**
2 tablespoons **vin santo** or **sweet Marsala**
4 drops of **vanilla extract**
1½ tablespoons **caster sugar**
175 g (6 oz) **plain flour**, plus extra for dusting
sunflower oil, for deep-frying
icing sugar, for dusting

Put the egg, salt, vin santo or Marsala, vanilla extract and caster sugar in a food processor and pulse until combined. Add the flour and pulse again until you have a firm dough. Knead on a work surface for 2 minutes until smooth and elastic.

Set a pasta machine at the largest opening. Cut the dough into 3 rectangular pieces. Run 1 rectangle through the machine. Fold in half widthways and run through again. Lower the setting by 1 notch and run the dough through again, then run once through each of the remaining settings. If the sheet becomes too long to handle, cut in half and run 1 half through at a time. If it becomes too sticky, dust with a little flour.

Lay the sheet on a surface dusted with flour and cover with a clean tea towel while you roll out the remaining dough. Use a sharp knife to cut the dough sheets into 3.5 cm (1½ inch) lengths.

Heat enough oil for deep-frying in a deep saucepan to 180–190°C (350–375°F), or until a cube of bread browns in 30 seconds. Add the ribbons, in batches, and cook for 30 seconds until golden all over. Drain on kitchen paper. Leave to cool completely, then generously dust with icing sugar. The ribbons can be stored in an airtight container for up to 2 days.

For honey & cinnamon pastry ribbons, replace the caster sugar with 1 tablespoon honey and use 1 teaspoon ground cinnamon instead of the vanilla extract. Prepare and cook as above.

watermelon & choc-chip sorbet

Serves **4–6**
Preparation time **20 minutes**, plus chilling and freezing
Cooking time **5 minutes**

750 g (1½ lb) **peeled watermelon**, deseeded and cubed
300 g (10 oz) **caster sugar**
8 tablespoons **lemon juice**
pink food colouring (optional)
1 **egg white**
125 g (4 oz) **chocolate chips**

Purée the watermelon in a food processor or blender. Add the sugar and process for 30 seconds.

Pour into a saucepan and bring slowly to the boil, stirring until the sugar has dissolved, then simmer for 1 minute. Remove from the heat, add the lemon juice, then leave to cool, adding a few drops of pink food colouring, if liked. Chill for at least 1 hour or overnight.

Use an ice-cream machine for the best results. Half-freeze the mixture according to the manufacturer's instructions, then lightly whisk the egg white and add with the motor running still running. Stir in the chocolate chips, then transfer to a plastic freezerproof container and freeze until firm.

Alternatively, freeze the mixture in a shallow freezer tray until frozen around the edges, then mash well with a fork. Whisk the egg white until stiff in a bowl. Drop spoonfuls of the sorbet into the egg white while whisking constantly with a hand-held electric whisk until the mixture is thick and foamy. Return to the freezer to firm up, then stir in the chocolate chips when almost frozen. Freeze until firm.

Transfer the sorbet to the refrigerator for 20 minutes before serving to soften. Serve with dessert biscuits.

For watermelon & orange sorbet, omit the cinnamon and chocolate chips. Reduce the quantity of watermelon to 500 g (1 lb) and process to a purée. Heat the sugar in a pan with 250 ml (8 fl oz) freshly squeezed orange juice, stirring until dissolved. Once cooled combine the watermelon, sweetened orange juice and lemon juice. Freeze as above.

frozen bellini

Serves **4**
Preparation time **15 minutes**

750 g (1½ lb) **ripe peaches**, stoned
100 ml (3½ fl oz) **sweet sparkling wine**
juice of ½ **lemon**
1 tablespoon **icing sugar**, plus extra to taste
15 **ice cubes**

Put 500 g (1 lb) of the peaches in a blender and blend to a purée. Transfer to a large bowl. Slice the remaining fruit, put in a separate bowl and gently toss with the wine.

Whizz the lemon juice, icing sugar and ice cubes in the blender until the ice is well crushed – you may need to do this in stages to avoid overheating the blender.

Transfer the crushed ice mixture to the bowl with the fruit and stir well to combine thoroughly. Taste, adding more icing sugar if necessary, and serve immediately, topped with the sliced fruit.

For cheat's strawberry & balsamic granita, replace the peaches with 625 g (1¼ lb) strawberries, hulled. Purée 500 g (1 lb) of the strawberries, then quarter the remaining strawberries and stir into 2 tablespoons aged balsamic vinegar, instead of the sparkling wine. Complete the recipe as above.

pistachio & pine nut biscotti

Makes **50**
Preparation time **20 minutes**, plus cooling
Cooking time **50 minutes–1 hour**

175 g (6 oz) **shelled pistachio nuts**
2 tablespoons **pine nuts**
125 g (4 oz) **unsalted butter**, softened, plus extra for greasing
200 g (7 oz) **granulated sugar**
2 **eggs**, beaten
finely grated **rind** of 1 **lemon**
1 tablespoon **Amaretto di Saronno**
about 375 g (12 oz) **plain flour**, plus extra for dusting
1½ teaspoons **baking powder**
½ teaspoon **salt**
75 g (3 oz) **coarse polenta**

Spread the pistachios and pine nuts out on a baking sheet and toast in a preheated oven, 160°C (325°F), Gas Mark 3, for 5–10 minutes until golden. Remove the nuts and leave to cool but leave the oven on.

Beat the butter and sugar together in a large bowl until just mixed, then beat in the eggs, lemon rind and Amaretto. Sift the flour, baking powder and salt together into a separate bowl, then stir into the butter mixture with the polenta. Stir in the toasted pistachios and pine nuts.

Turn the dough out on to a floured work surface and knead until smooth, working in a little more flour if too sticky. Divide into quarters and roll each quarter into a sausage 5 cm (2 inches) long and 1.5 cm (¾ inch) thick. Flatten slightly. Place on 2 greased baking sheets and bake in the oven for about 35 minutes until just golden around the edges.

Leave to cool slightly, then cut on the diagonal into 1 cm (½ inch) thick slices. Place, cut-side down, on the baking sheets and bake for a further 10–15 minutes until golden brown and crisp, being careful not to burn. Transfer to a wire rack to cool.

For almond & chocolate biscotti, replace the pistachios and pine nuts with 200 g (7 oz) blanched almonds and toast them as above. When adding the almonds to the biscuit dough also include 100 g (3½ oz) roughly chopped plain chocolate. Shape and bake as above.

index

almonds: almond & chocolate biscotti 234
almond biscuits 218
chocolate & nut panettone 224
chocolate, almond & prune parfaits 208
fennel & almond soup 104
pear & almond cake 212
anchovies 9
crudités & garlic anchovy dip 50
apricots: apricot jam tart 206
caramel panna cotta & apricots 214
arancini 30
artichokes: braised artichokes & potatoes 186
prosciutto & artichoke sfincione 80
stuffed peppers 46
asparagus: asparagus & pancetta risotto 116
asparagus, pea & mint risotto 116
cheesy prosciutto-wrapped asparagus 40
pasta salad with mozzarella & asparagus 74
spaghetti with charred asparagus 74
aubergines: aubergine & courgette parmigiana 180
aubergine, basil & ricotta pizza 84
with pancetta & sage 190
Sicilian caponata 188

barley, bean & porcini soup 92
basil: basil & lemon batter 18
basil & tomato focaccia 86
batter: basil & lemon 18
fried vegetables in 18
beans 12
mixed bean salad 44
see also broad beans, cannellini beans etc
beef: arancini 30
beef in red wine 170
classic meatloaf 152
devilled fillet steaks 164
meatballs in red wine sauce 152
meatballs with spaghetti 70
oxtail in red wine with tomatoes 170
steak sandwich with red pesto 162
Bellini, frozen 232
biscuits: almond & chocolate biscotti 234
almond biscuits 218
candied fruit & sultana biscuits 218
pistachio & pine nut biscotti 234
blackberry & lemon tiramisu 222
borlotti beans: barley, bean & porcini soup 92
borlotti, pasta & red mullet soup 92
braised black cabbage & borlotti 198
tuna & borlotti bean salad 44
bread: mozzarella in carrozza 38
spiced Parma ham & mozzarella in carrozza 38
tomato & bread soup 102
tomato, onion & bread salad 142
see also bruschetta; focaccia
broad bean bruschetta 24
broccoli, orecchiette with 54
bruschetta: broad bean 24
Parmesan & cannellini bean 24
Parmesan, porcini & radicchio 20
porcini bruschetta with truffle oil 20

cabbage, black see cavolo nero
cake, pear & almond 212
calves' liver & caramelized onions 154
candied fruit & sultana biscuits 218
cannellini beans: cannellini with pancetta & rosemary 184
cannellini with sage & tomato 184
Parmesan & cannellini bean bruschetta 24
ribollita 106
capers 10
caper & lemon peperonata 194
caponata: potato & pepper 188
Sicilian 188
caramel panna cotta & apricots 214
carpaccio of fresh tuna 26
cauliflower, penne with 54
cavolo nero: braised black cabbage & borlotti 198
ribollita 106
cheese 10–11
aubergine & courgette parmigiana 180
baked polenta with Gorgonzola 120
cheesy polenta & mushrooms 124
courgette & smoked mozzarella pizza 84
courgette, pea & cheese frittata 196
fennel & olive parmigiana 180
grilled radicchio, Fontina & speck 182
mozzarella & rocket pizza rolls 88
mozzarella in carrozza 38
onion, Gorgonzola & walnut pizza 76
Parmesan & cannellini bean bruschetta
Parmesan crisps 96
Parmesan, porcini & radicchio bruschetta 20
pasta salad with mozzarella & asparagus 74
pizza fiorentina 78
pizza with smoked mozzarella, Parma ham & rocket 82
pizza with speck & dolcelatte 82
potato & cheese pizza 76
potato & green bean bake 200
spiced Parma ham & mozzarella in carrozza 38
tomato & mozzarella arancini 30
see also mascarpone; ricotta
chestnut, rice & pancetta soup 94
chicken: chicken breast with rosemary & pancetta 158
chicken Milanese 174
chicken with olives & rosemary 166
devilled chicken breasts 164
roast chicken with herbs & garlic 176
roast chicken with lemon & sage 176
chicken liver & caramelized onions 154

chips, polenta 122
chocolate: almond & chocolate biscotti 234
  chocolate, almond & prune parfaits 208
  chocolate & hazelnut parfaits 208
  chocolate & nut panettone 224
  chocolate & raspberry jam tart 206
  chocolate & ricotta tart 210
  chocolate sorbet 220
  hazelnut chzocolate ice cream 226
  rum & chocolate-chip sorbet 220
  speedy chunky chocolate ice cream 226
  watermelon & choc-chip sorbet 230
citrus peel panna cotta 214
clams 14
  clam & courgette soup 108
  spaghetti with clams & chilli 60
  spaghetti with clams, pancetta & tomatoes 60
cod: cod & lentils in tomato sauce 172
  see also salt cod
coffee: classic tiramisu 222
  coffee-cream liqueur panna cotta 204
  zabaglione semifreddo with coffee 216
courgettes: aubergine & courgette parmigiana 180
  braised courgettes, peas & prosciutto 186
  clam & courgette soup 108
  courgette & smoked mozzarella pizza 84
  courgette, pea & cheese frittata 196
  griddled courgettes with lemon, mint & Parmesan 42
  prawn, courgette & saffron risotto 118
  spiced king prawn & courgette soup 108
cream: panna cotta 204, 214
crudités & garlic anchovy dip 50

devilled chicken breasts 164
devilled fillet steaks 164
dips 50, 122

eggs: courgette, pea & cheese frittata 196
  spinach & pea frittata 196
equipment 13–14

fennel: fennel & almond soup 104
  fennel & olive parmigiana 180
  fennel, lemon & thyme sea bass in a salt crust 128
  fennel, rice & pancetta soup 94
  fennel soup with olive gremolata 104
  sardines stuffed with fennel 136
fettuccine: fettuccine & dried porcini sauce 66
  fettuccine with creamy mushroom & tarragon sauce 66
figs: balsamic figs with Parma ham 28
focaccia: basil & tomato 86
  olive, onion & rosemary 86
frittata: courgette, pea & cheese 196
  spinach & pea 196
fusilli with tuna, capers & mint 58

garlic: garlic & caper mayonnaise 50
  garlic in basil & chilli oil 36
  garlic cloves in olive oil 36
  toasted garlic & chilli oil 100
gnocchi: rocket 72
  spinach potato 72
granita, cheat's strawberry & balsamic 232
green beans: potato & green bean bake 200
grissini, prosciutto-wrapped 40

ham see Parma ham; prosciutto
hazelnuts: chocolate & hazelnut parfaits 208
  hazelnut chocolate ice cream 226
honey & cinnamon pastry ribbons 228

ice cream: hazelnut chocolate 226
  speedy chunky chocolate 226

lamb: lamb cutlets with red pesto 162
  lamb shanks braised in milk 160
  leg of lamb with lemon & rosemary 156
  roast lamb with wine & juniper 156
  lasagne: mushroom, blue cheese & spinach 56
  wild mushroom 56
lemon: lemon & ricotta tart 210
  lemon panna cotta & raspberries 204
  lemon, rocket & basil linguine 68
lentils 12
  cod & lentils in tomato sauce 172
  sausage & lentils in tomato sauce 172
linguine, lemon, rocket & basil 68
liver: calves' liver & caramelized onions 154
  chicken liver & caramelized onions 154

mackerel see smoked mackerel
Marsala: mascarpone, Marsala & orange cream 212
  zabaglione semifreddo with coffee 216
mascarpone: classic tiramisu 222
  mascarpone, Marsala & orange cream 212
  squash with mascarpone & sage 190
mayonnaise, garlic & caper 50
meatballs in red wine sauce 152
meatballs with spaghetti 70
meatloaf, classic 152
melon: minted melon with Parma ham 28
monkfish: monkfish in salsa d'agrumi 138
  roast garlic-studded monkfish 132
  roasted monkfish with olive paste 132
mozzarella & rocket pizza rolls 88
mozzarella in carrozza 38
mushrooms 13
  cheesy polenta & mushrooms 124
  fettuccine & dried porcini sauce 66
  fettuccine with creamy mushroom & tarragon sauce 66
  mushroom, blue cheese & spinach lasagne 56
  Parmesan, porcini & radicchio bruschetta 20
  porcini bruschetta with truffle oil 20
  wild mushroom lasagne 56

mussels 14
  mussels alla marinara 144
  rocket & garlic crumbed mussels 22

olive oil 11
  garlic in basil & chilli oil 36
  garlic cloves in olive oil 36
  toasted garlic & chilli oil 100
olives: fennel soup with olive gremolata 104
  olive, onion & rosemary focaccia 86
  roasted monkfish with olive paste 132
onions: calves' liver & caramelized onions 154
  chicken liver & caramelized onions 154
  olive, onion & rosemary focaccia 86
  onion, Gorgonzola & walnut pizza 76
orange: mascarpone, Marsala & orange cream 212
  watermelon & orange sorbet 230
orecchiette with broccoli 54
oxtail in red wine with tomatoes 170

pancetta: asparagus & pancetta risotto 116
  aubergines with pancetta & sage 190
  cannellini with pancetta & rosemary 184
  pancetta, potato & fregola soup 98
  roasted tomato & pancetta pasta 64
  roasted tomato, pancetta & spinach salad 64
panettone 224
  chocolate & nut 224
panna cotta: caramel panna cotta & apricots 214
  citrus peel panna cotta 214
  coffee-cream liqueur panna cotta 204
  lemon panna cotta & raspberries 204

Parma ham 11
  balsamic figs with 28
  minted melon with 28
  spiced Parma ham & mozzarella in carrozza 38
  veal escalopes with 158
Parmesan & cannellini bean bruschetta 24
Parmesan crisps 96
Parmesan, porcini & radicchio bruschetta 20
pasta 11–12
  pasta salad with mozzarella & asparagus 74
  roasted tomato & pancetta pasta 64
  see also cannelloni, spaghetti *etc*
pastry ribbons 228
  honey & cinnamon 228
pâté, salt cod 34
peaches: frozen Bellini 232
pear & almond cake 212
peas: courgette, pea & cheese frittata 196
  spinach & pea frittata 196
  tortellini with lemon, pea & basil sauce 68
penne: with creamy cauliflower 54
  with grilled vegetables, capers & mint 58
  peperonata, caper & lemon 194
peppers: grilled peppers in herb oil 46
  peperonata 194
  pork meatballs in a tomato & red pepper sauce 70
  potato & pepper caponata 188
  potatoes with red peppers & olives 192
  stuffed peppers 46
pesto, red: lamb cutlets with 162
  steak sandwich with 162
pine nuts: pistachio & pine nut biscotti 234
  spinach with 198
pistachio & pine nut biscotti 234
pizzas: aubergine, basil & ricotta pizza 84
  basic pizza dough 15
  cherry tomato & rocket pizza 88
  courgette & smoked mozzarella pizza 84

mozzarella & rocket pizza rolls 88
  onion, Gorgonzola & walnut pizza 76
  pizza fiorentina 78
  potato & cheese pizza 76
  prosciutto & artichoke sfincione 80
  spinach, anchovy & caper pizza 78
  tomato, onion & anchovy sfincione 80
  with smoked mozzarella, Parma ham & rocket 82
  with speck & dolcelatte 82
polenta 12
  baked polenta with Gorgonzola 120
  cheesy polenta & mushrooms 124
  griddled herbed polenta 120
  polenta chips 122
porcini bruschetta with truffle oil 20
pork: pork braised in milk 160
  pork meatballs in a tomato & red pepper sauce 70
  roast herbed pork belly 168
  sausage & apricot stuffed pork 168
potatoes: braised artichokes & potatoes 186
  garlicky potatoes with tomatoes 192
  potato & cheese pizza 76
  potato & green bean bake 200
  potato & pepper caponata 188
  potato, olive & sunblush tomato bake 200
  smoked mackerel with potato & salsa verde salad 130
  spinach potato gnocchi 72
  with red peppers & olives 192
prawns: barbecued prawn skewers 142
  prawn, courgette & saffron risotto 118
  spiced king prawn & courgette soup 108
  spicy fried prawns 148
prosciutto: braised courgettes, peas & prosciutto 186
  cheesy prosciutto-wrapped asparagus 40

prosciutto & artichoke sfincione 80
prosciutto-wrapped grissini 40
prunes: chocolate, almond & prune parfaits 208
pumpkin: pumpkin & garlic soup 96
  pumpkin risotto with amaretto biscuits & almonds 114
  pumpkin, sage & chilli risotto 114

rabbit in white wine & rosemary 166
radicchio: grilled radicchio, Fontina & speck 182
  grilled radicchio with walnut vinaigrette 182
  radicchio risotto with pancetta 110
raspberries: lemon panna cotta & raspberries 204
  zabaglione semifreddos with raspberry sauce 216
red mullet: borlotti, pasta & red mullet soup 92
  with salsa verde 130
ribollita 106
rice 13
  seafood rice salad 48
  tomatoes stuffed with rice 112
  see also risotto
ricotta: aubergine, basil & ricotta pizza 84
  baked ricotta with bay leaves 32
  baked ricotta with rocket, Parmesan & lemon 32
  chocolate & ricotta tart 210
  lemon & ricotta tart 210
risotto: arancini 30
  asparagus & pancetta 116
  asparagus, pea & mint 116
  prawn, courgette & saffron 118
  pumpkin, sage & chilli 114
  pumpkin with amaretto biscuits & almonds 114
  radicchio with pancetta 110
  saffron 118
  tomato & mozzarella arancini 30
  watercress & lemon 110
rocket: baked ricotta with rocket, Parmesan & lemon 32
  cherry tomato & rocket pizza 88
  lemon, rocket & basil linguine 68

rocket & garlic crumbed mussels 22
rocket & tomato tagliatelle 62
rocket gnocchi 72
rum & chocolate-chip sorbet 220

saffron risotto 118
salads: mixed bean salad 44
  pasta salad with mozzarella & asparagus 74
  roasted tomato, pancetta & spinach salad 64
  seafood rice salad 48
  seafood salad 48
  smoked mackerel with potato & salsa verde salad 130
  tomato, onion & bread salad 142
  tuna & borlotti bean salad 44
salsa verde, red mullet with 130
salt cod: salt cod in batter 34
  salt cod pâté 34
sardines: sardines stuffed with fennel 136
  with sardine & fennel sauce 136
sausage & apricot stuffed pork 168
sausage & lentils in tomato sauce 172
scallops, tomato & parsley crumbed 22
sea bass in a salt crust 128
seafood: seafood & fregola soup 98
  seafood rice salad 48
  seafood salad 48
semifreddo, zabaglione 216
Sicilian caponata 188
smoked mackerel with potato & salsa verde salad 130
sole: sole in lemon & basil sauce 138
  with lemon, parsley & garlic 134
  with tomatoes & capers 134
sorbets: chocolate 220
  rum & chocolate-chip 220
  watermelon & choc-chip 230
  watermelon & orange 230
soups: barley, bean & porcini 92
  borlotti, pasta & red mullet 92
  chestnut, rice & pancetta 94
  clam & courgette 108
  fennel & almond 104
  fennel, rice & pancetta 94

fennel soup with olive gremolata 104
pancetta, potato & fregola 98
pumpkin & garlic 96
ribollita 106
roasted tomato, bread & balsamic 102
seafood & fregola 98
spiced king prawn & courgette 108
spring ribollita 106
tomato & bread 102
white bean 100
spaghetti: meatballs with 70
  with charred asparagus 74
  with clams & chilli 60
  with clams, pancetta & tomatoes 60
  with sardine & fennel sauce 136
speck: grilled radicchio, Fontina & speck 182
  pizza with speck & dolcelatte 82
spinach: mushroom, blue cheese & spinach lasagne 56
  pizza fiorentina 78
  roasted tomato, pancetta & spinach salad 64
  spinach, anchovy & caper pizza 78
  spinach & pea frittata 196
  spinach potato gnocchi 72
  with pine nuts 198
spring ribollita 106
squash with mascarpone & sage 190
squid 14
  barbecued stuffed squid 146
  fried calamari 148
  squid alla marinara 144
  stuffed squid in tomato sauce 146
steak sandwich with red pesto 162
strawberries: cheat's strawberry & balsamic granita 232
sweet pastry ribbons 228
swordfish: fresh swordfish carpaccio 26
  with onion & sultanas 140

tagliatelle: rocket & tomato 62
  tomato & pancetta 62
tarts: apricot jam tart 206
  chocolate & raspberry jam tart 206

chocolate & ricotta tart 210
lemon & ricotta tart 210
tiramisu 222
blackberry & lemon 222
tomatoes 13
cannellini with sage & tomato 184
cherry tomato & rocket pizza 88
cod & lentils in tomato sauce 172
garlicky potatoes with tomatoes 192
oxtail in red wine with tomatoes 170
peperonata 194
pork meatballs in a tomato & red pepper sauce 70
potato, olive & sunblush tomato bake 200
roasted tomato & pancetta pasta 64
roasted tomato, bread & balsamic soup 102
roasted tomato, pancetta & spinach salad 64
rocket & tomato tagliatelle 62
sausage & lentils in tomato sauce 172

Sicilian caponata 188
sole with tomatoes & capers 134
stuffed squid in tomato sauce 146
tomato & basil dip 122
tomato & bread soup 102
tomato & mozzarella arancini 30
tomato & pancetta tagliatelle 62
tomato & parsley crumbed scallops 22
tomato, onion & anchovy sfincione 80
tomato, onion & bread salad 142
tomatoes stuffed with rice 112
tomatoes stuffed with rice, capers, anchovies & olives 112
tortellini with lemon, pea & basil sauce 68
tuna: carpaccio of fresh tuna 26
fusilli with tuna, capers & mint 58
tuna & borlotti bean salad 44
with onion & olives 140
turkey Milanese 174

veal escalopes with Parma ham 158
vegetables: crudités & garlic anchovy dip 50
fried vegetables in batter 18
griddled vegetable platter 42
penne with grilled vegetables, capers & mint 58
vinaigrette, walnut 182
vinegar 13

walnut vinaigrette 182
watercress & lemon risotto 110
watermelon: watermelon & choc-chip sorbet 230
watermelon & orange sorbet 230
white bean soup 100

zabaglione semifreddo 216

acknowledgements

Executive Editor Nicky Hill
Editor Kerenza Swift
Executive Art Editor Geoff Fennel
Designer Joanna MacGregor
Photographer Stephen Conroy
Home Economist Marina Filippelli
Props Stylist Liz Hippisley
Production Controller Carolin Stransky

Special photography: © Octopus Publishing Group Ltd/Stephen Conroy

Other Photography: © Octopus Publishing Group Ltd